CW01202473

Ma Ma Hta
Burmese Headwoman - 1940's

This biography will surprise you. Ma Ma Hta - pronounced Mama Ta' - shows unique strength of character, which will arouse interest and astonish you.

Mama Ta' belonged to a large, educated family (with a father who read 'The Times' every morning). We see them involved in coping with an influx of Japanese invaders - during WW2.

The Japanese appointed her to be a Headwoman at the age of twenty-eight. Yet, never afraid of them - she controlled and disciplined their unruly troops (It makes you laugh!) ... Later she even prevented her imminent execution ....

But that's not all!

By the same author

Bougainvillea (Wartime India)

MA MA HTA

Burmese Headwoman – 1940s

Denise Macdonald

Denise Macdonald

19-10-02

**OM
publishing**

Copyright © 2001 Denise Macdonald

First Published in 2001 by Paternoster Press

07 06 05 04 03 02 01 7 6 5 4 3 2 1

OM Publishing is an imprint of Paternoster Publishing,
P.O. Box 300, Carlisle, Cumbria, CA3 0QS, UK
and P.O. Box 1047, Waynesboro, GA 30830-2047, USA
www.paternoster-publishing.com

The right of Denise Macdonald to be identified as the Author
of this Work has been asserted by her in accordance with the
Copyright, Designs and Patents Act 1988.

*All rights reserved. No part of this publication may be reproduced,
stored in a retrieval system, or transmitted in any form or by any
means, electronic, mechanical, photocopying, recording or otherwise,
without the prior permission of the publisher or a licence permitting
restricted copying. In the UK such licences are issued by the
Copyright Licensing Agency,
90 Tottenham Court Road, London W1P 9HE.*

British Library Cataloguing in Publication Data
A catalogue record for this book is available from the British
Library

ISBN 1-85078-372-1

Cover Design by Campsie
Typeset by WestKey Ltd, Falmouth, Cornwall
Printed in Great Britain by Omnia Books Ltd,
Bishopbriggs, Glasgow G64

Contents

Acknowledgements

It has been a great pleasure to be with Ma Ma Hta during the writing of this book, which contains some things that she has never divulged even to her close family. I am also grateful to Babs and Norman Martinesz and their daughter, Kay, for welcoming me into their home so that I was able to spend time with Ma Ma Hta.

Author's Note

BURMA (Myanmar) seems to be a relatively unknown country. Therefore I considered it necessary, in this biography, to go into some detail about the land, its people and its more recent history, so that the reader will get the picure of Ma Ma Hta's Burmese background, and of what was going on around her as the story progresses. The Preface sets the Burma scene. The Appendix presents a fuller portrayal of contemporary Burmese politics and events in the war.

If one visits Myanmar today, it appears to be a mainly Buddhist country. Everywhere there are temples, pagodas, statues of Buddha, shrines upon its picturesque hills, and monasteries from whence emerge saffron-robed monks who are still respected. Buddhist festivals are enjoyed and traditional 'theatre' is full of drama, song and dance – exclusive to Burma.

Outsiders have thought that Burma is like a country set in a time warp.

But is it?

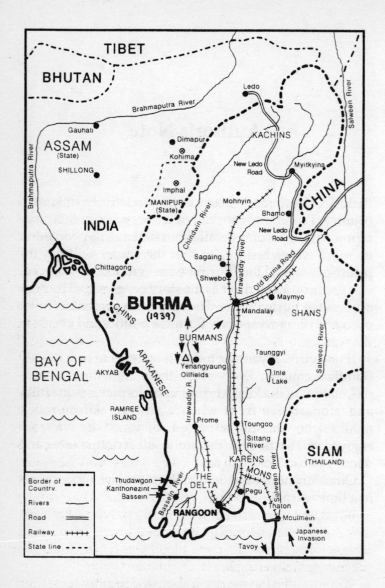

A Bird's-eye View of Burma – 1939

Preface

When you hear the word 'Burma' – what comes to mind? Maybe you've heard of Burmah Oil, or that white and green jade stone is found there – or you connect Burma with the renowned leader Aung San, and his daughter Aung San Suu Kyi. Perhaps you worked there years ago in the Civil Service or in business, or sweated through Burmese jungles during the Burma Campaign of World War 2. Or are you one of the Burmese nationals who have settled here in Britain, and are pleased to see something of your country on television or in the newspapers these days?

To begin with it may be useful to get our bearings in a miniature overview.

Burma is shaped like a simple kite, with the long streaming 'tail' of Tenasserim State tapering southwards for 500 miles. There are four major rivers, the Chindwin, Irrawaddy, Sittang and Salween, which have their sources in the horseshoe of high northern hills. The lengthy Irrawaddy appears to cut the country in half; a huge oilfield as well as historically important towns lie along its banks; it resembles the aorta blood vessel which plays a key role in delivering life to the human body.

Authors who have written about the country have been much impressed, not only with the land features, but by the Burmese people, who seem to have woven a spell of enchantment over them.

We are about to take a round trip of Burma in 1939. We fly in with the birds, from Singapore; travelling northwards over her southernmost border, at Victoria Point we see teak forests, rubber plantations, housing for tin-miners, fruit trees and oyster beds of cultured pearls at Tavoy, which is amongst 'Malay' fishing villages spaced along beaches of white sand. Passing on to the town of Moulmein (near which Ma Ma Hta's parents were born, and cultural centre of the go-ahead *Mons* people), there is much activity including boat-building, saw-milling, ship-loading and market gardening for other parts of Burma and the world.

Looking northeastwards, we see distant hills, gorges and waterfalls, whence gush the turbulent waters of the longest river, the Salween. Nearer Moulmein it sluggishly pushes immense rafts of floating logs down to the ports before expending itself in the brilliant sea.

Flying due west, over the Gulf of Martaban, we are soon above the dry docks and gleaming oil refineries at Syriam as we approach the capital of Burma, Rangoon (Yangon). It is a surprisingly green city on Burma's southern shoreline: parkland, lakes, gardens, avenues; also Government buildings, houses, flatlets, shops, stately liners at the wharves – all dwarfed by the towering golden Shwedagon pagoda. This is where Ma Ma Hta works.

Continuing over thick, steamy jungle, muddy swamps and extensive paddy-fields of the Irradwaddy Delta region, we come to the thriving rice-exporting port of *Bassein*, with its surrounding Burman and Karen villages. Ma Ma Hta's home is in this area.

Veering north-westwards along the hill-backed, islanded coast of the Arakan Peninsula, we fly towards the border with India. General W. Slim wrote of this region, that the hills were 'jungle-clad, with clinging, tightly-packed greenery .... razor-edged ridges covered to their very summits with the densest jungle'.

The *Arakanese* have a lot in common with the Indians across the border. Their coastline is one of swaying palms, tempting strands, casuarina trees and rocky volcanic islets set in a glittering turquoise Andaman Sea.

Now flying due north, we see wooded hills and isolated villages. These are the Chin Hills, where the fearless *Chin* people live.

Then, turning in an easterly direction, we proceed across expansive, low-lying jungle, then across the hot, dry plains of Central Burma. This is where most of the historically powerful Burmans have their home ('Burmese' is the term for all of Burma's citizens). Looking towards the south from here, on a clear day we may just be able to make out the immense flatland of the ancient kingdom of Pagan with thousands of crumbling pagodas, temples and monasteries strewn across it, including some large, solid, renovated pagodas. Beyond them rises volcanic Mt. Popa – reputed to be the home of the popular folklore's *nats* (good and bad spirits), and hordes of monkeys and of Burma's distinctive brown cobra.

We bypass Mandalay (to be dealt with later in the book) – the famous town, which came into existence through the visionary King Mindon, who planned that it should be a kind of 'Centre of the World'.

Further east is the hill-station of Maymyo. In the foothills of the Shan Plateau at 3,510 feet, Maymyo has government buildings: colonial-type residences for Government, Army and Civil Service personnel. There are tennis and squash courts, golf courses, fine teak Burmese houses and smaller homes for Indian and Nepali workers. Horsedrawn coaches share the roads with modern vehicles. Rhododendrons grow amongst the oaks and pines.

Flying northwards over the mining area of Mogok, famed for jade, rare rubies and other precious and semi-precious stones, we pass *Mohnyin* (where Ma Ma Hta would bring evacuee children during the War).

Only another 100 miles to Myitkyina,which is the rail terminus for trains from Rangoon. In the extreme north are the Kachin Hills, inhabited by the courageous *Kachin* people. Beyond are the Himalayas and China.

We fly over the upper reaches of the Irrawaddy, seeing an enormous number of floating logs, and go southwards, above wild hills of rich forests of teak and other rare hardwoods, to the frontier town of Bhamo. It is a kaleidoscope of colourful markets crowded with traders and animal caravans, who have brought Chinese silks and materials, medicinal herbs and maybe opium, into Burma; receiving salt, cotton, jade and a variety of goods to take back to inland China.

Leaving Bhamo behind, hill tracts seem wilder and the scenery more spectacular; high mountains and deep chasms through which the Salween will continue to cascade over rocks and rocky defiles for 500 miles before reaching Moulmein.

We are nearing the end of our flight now: still going south and keeping parallel with the eastern border between Burma and Siam (Thailand) – heading for the Shan Plateau, 3,000 feet above sea level. The *Shan* people are industrious. As we enter their airspace, blast furnaces of the zinc, lead and silver mines come into view. Further on, foresters are felling teak trees, under strict supervision with due regard to the general environment. On the plateau, in the scattered villages are weaving sheds, where a variety of goods are made – including Shan shoulderbags, used by many Burmese women and men, and exported to India and other places.

The main town of Taunggyi, at 4,000 feet, nestles in

jungle-covered hills, with brown plains and blue and purple hills in the distance. It looks attractive, with its Shan Parliament House, government offices, the Commissioner's residence, dwellings and shops – all set amongst flowering trees.

On the two-mile long Inle Lake on the plain just south of Taunggyi, a Shan Festival happens to be in full swing! Thousands of exuberant spectators are encouraging their favourite couple of leg-rowers – as boats jostle dangerously. Each craft, rather like a punt, is propelled forward by two men – one fore and one aft – who work an oar, skilfully holding it with an arm and one leg. A great roar of approval greets the winners.

Flying now along the course of the widening Salween and above districts where there is tungsten and rich forests of valuable trees, we pass over Kayah State into the Pegu area. Many *Karens* live there. They are a hardworking people who are also to be found throughout Lower Burma, among the Burmans, Mons, British, Indians and Chinese.

The round trip comes to an end at Rangoon.

1

Introductions

The Japanese interrogation officer was almost beside himself with rage. He glared at the slight, calm, upright figure of the Burmese woman before him then looked at the interpreter and said between clenched teeth: 'I have been all over Burma – north, south, east and west – but no one has ever dared to speak to me like this one!' The translator beside him remained silent.

The two Karen girls, listening behind the door, were terrified for Ma Ma Hta.

'Why did she say that to him?' whispered one.

'They are sure to punish her!' replied the other, shaking with terror.

This particular incident took place during the occupation of Burma by the Japanese Imperial Army in the early 1940s, when it was much safer for nationals to maintain a very low profile.

* * * * *

The Japanese had appointed Ma Ma Hta (pronounced *Ma-Ma Tah*) as the village headwoman – in charge of about two hundred families – in place of her ailing father. At the Banquet given in honour of a visiting Japanese General, she had been very outspoken. Ordered to present herself at the office the following day, she found that she was to be interrogated.

The interrogator suspected her of being a spy – but that was not all: there was another reason for cross-examining her ....

However, it is too soon to let you into Ma Ma Hta's secrets.

* * * * *

We first met Ma Ma Hta Thin in the 1980s when she came to live in London for a few years. Her house backed onto ours. Speaking to her over the garden fence, we found her warm and friendly. She and her semi-invalid husband, Major Hla Thin, cared for students, friends and acquaintances from many countries and we were among those invited into their home.

One day, while exchanging details of our past lives, an unusual thing happened. Ma Ma Hta told a little story with regard to her working days – which caused her to 'let slip' an intriguing confrontation which she had had with the Japanese military, when they had occupied her country during the Second World War. I was fascinated and, rightly or wrongly, pressed her for more information. She certainly wouldn't have volunteered anything otherwise.

Eventually it was suggested that it would be good to make a record of what proved to be a series of amazing incidents in a possible biography. The deciding factor was that, after much deliberation, Ma Ma Hta said: 'Yes, maybe now is the time that those things can be made known.'

Home in Lower Burma

It was early 1941. Ma Ma Hta was on holiday. She was back home, in the tropical-leaved suburbs of the thriving, modern port of Bassein in Lower Burma. She enjoyed every moment of being with her much-loved elderly father and mother, together with their large family. Basically she was never so happy as when she was with them in the beautiful natural surroundings of Kanthonezint.

Her father, U Chit Htwe (pronounced *oo chit tway*) and his wife Daw Ma Ma had, on his retirement as Headmaster of a large Middle School in Bassein, bought some land in a verdant district, popular with professionals who lived comfortably in 'pukka' bungalows of whitewashed brick with red-tiled roofs or in attractive wooden homes. Nearby was a small Buddhist monastery. Just the other side of the main road to Bassein was a traditional Burmese village. This suburban area was known as Kanthonezint – where three small lakes joined – and there was enough land for each householder to cultivate.

U Chit Htwe had purchased a smallholding of about ten acres and built a house large enough for several people: his own family of nine children, a daughter's baby, one son's elderly mother-in-law, a deaf Burmese girl, an adopted orphaned deaf Chinese girl, and various

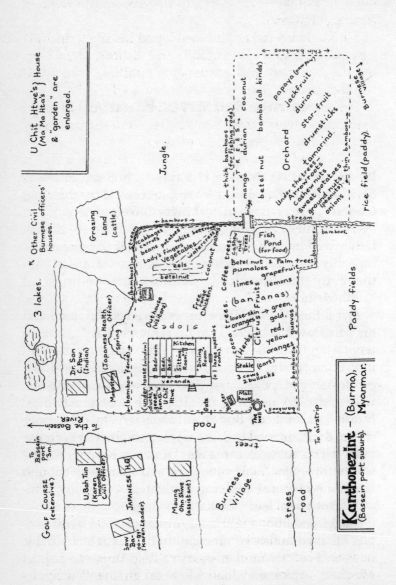

Karthonezint – (Burma),
(Bassein port suburb). Myanmar.

'helpers' who lived in and were not exactly servants. All lived as 'family' – according to the custom of extended families in Burma.

Ma Ma Hta's father had developed his site to include two outhouses for extra friends and visitors, and a barn for the cowman and gardener's families, who lived together as one. There was also a cowshed.

There were days when Ma Ma Hta and her father sat together in their fairly large sitting-cum-dining room, occupied with paperwork or reading.

She looked across at him – enjoying that familiar, rather sweet expression on his face, as he went through his local daily English *Fair Play* newspaper, *The Times* and *The Guardian*. She was conscious that unlike her sisters, she herself hardly read a thing. She was much too busy; even now while she was trying to concentrate on a letter to her sweetheart, Hla (Hullar) Thin, there were so many other thoughts flitting through her lively mind!

Ma Ma Hta thought of her mother whom she could see walking slowly around their garden carefully examining the produce. It was sad that her mother was so frail these days – suffering from anaemia brought on by giving birth to twelve children (three of whom had died, leaving four boys and five girls). The helpers were really for her benefit: she was giving them excellent training in household duties and childcare. Ma Ma Hta was remembering how, before they had helpers, her mother had had to keep her away from school on and off for two to three years, so that she could lend a hand with the current babies. That was why Ma Ma Hta also felt inadequate educationally, compared with her clever sisters.

Ma Ma Hta thought of her earlier childhood when they had all lived in Bassein. Her father retired in 1933. While he was Headmaster of a large bustling American Baptist Mission School they had all lived in the Principal's rambling house in the big school compound. She had felt 'very free there'. There had been family discipline – 'very strict and no nonsense was tolerated – but there was plenty of fun and laughter'. Ma Ma Hta was proud of the fact that her father had become 'very well known and respected throughout the Bassein region'.

Ma Ma Hta loved being outside in their present compound. Their large, rear garden was in three sections: the first for a variety of vegetables, the second a plot for trees providing all types of citrus fruits, coffee beans and bananas. The third was a general orchard producing mangoes, durian fruit, cashew nuts, star fruit, papayas (paw paw), jackfruit and coconut, betel-nuts and 'drumsticks'. Underneath the trees there were onions, ordinary and sweet potatoes, arrowroots, groundnuts and different kinds of beans.

All these foods, plus the keeping of ducks, geese, American hens, home-reared freshwater pond fish and a couple of cows, meant that the family was almost self-sufficient – apart from having to buy or barter for oil, rice, meat and a few other commodities.

Every householder owned a well. Their big well, which was in the left-hand corner of the compound, happened to be the only freshwater one in the area fit for drinking. Her father had arranged his barbed wire fencing to run between the well and the house so that anyone passing along the road could use the well freely. Everyone knew that it had also gradually become the focal point for women to catch up on the local gossip, and for lads to meet girls!

The family referred to their immediate neighbourhood as 'the village', but villages in Burma were quite large.

Their 'village of Kanthonezint' was set in a very lush landscape. The whole scene was absolutely idyllic.

* * * * *

Whilst continuing to write her letter to Hla Thin, Ma Ma Hta was conscious of her father's presence. Besides reading, he kept himself busy by giving private tuition at home, providing free education for interested people, and for those who could not afford it; teaching arithmetic and English to nationals and the Burmese language to foreigners. He also gave her younger brother, Baba (*Bar bar*) extra lessons as he had not done as well as expected at school although he was the popular 'Number 1 goalie in the Bassein football team!' Her eldest sister also taught people at home. Ma Ma Hta and the rest of the family had felt the quiet influence of her father's godly life. She was pleased that he often spent time away from the house, caring for the outcasts of Burmese society, the unemployed, destitute and the gravediggers – sitting down with a gravedigger for a cup of tea and a chat was still taboo in Burma.

Ma Ma Hta got up to look out of the window overlooking the part of the garden to the right of the house; it was her 'favourite view'. Beneath clumps of bamboo bordering the compound, was a sparkling stream that flowed from a spring. At the water's edge there were three scented flowering trees, one or other of which bloomed all through the year. The *sagaphyu* tree produced waxy white blossoms continuously. To her it was symbolic of her Creator's continuing provision for the family as the thick white clusters were much in demand commercially, particularly by the Indians domiciled in Burma. The *sagaphyu* tree reminded her of Elijah's miraculous cruse of continually available oil for the widow at Zarephath, mentioned in the Old Testament.

Back at her letter-writing to Hla Thin, who was now a Captain in the British Army, she visualised him – tall, broad and handsome in his uniform – and then she pictured him looking distinguished in Burmese dress and wondered when she would see him again.

Yet, as a matter of fact, she was rather fed up with him! In his extremely regular weekly letters to her, she considered that he had too little to write; he didn't give much of what you might call news. She found his usual sentences, such as: 'How are you, my dear?' and 'I hope you are well. I am all right' – boring! Truth to tell, her own letters to him left something to be desired; they were too few and far between! This was partly due to the fact that she was much in demand but the underlying cause was that, although he was very much in love with her, she, at that time, did not feel the same.

Looking back, it seemed a long time since their first acquaintance in Rangoon. She remembered him coming later to Kanthonezint with one of her brothers, with whom he had become friendly. Ma Ma Hta was a tomboy at heart. Throughout her childhood she had played rough-and-tumble wildly energetic games with her brothers and their friends – yet she was still popular with the girls. To Hla Thin this aspect of her character was part of her charm. He found her strong, athletic and capable, in spite of ressembling a sprite, and his heart also warmed to her generosity of spirit shown in her daily, unselfconscious care for those around her.

She seemed older than her years. Because of her mother's fragility, and the fact that her elder sister ran the household most of the time, Ma Ma Hta had been called upon to shoulder the family's stresses and strains, even acting as nurse, at an abnormally early age. As the years passed, this training in a fairly hard 'school' had moulded her into a premature little 'mother' upon whom the younger members of the family could lean for support – especially when they wanted to get things done – rather than to expect them from their parents (their father had been frequently taken up with his school duties).

Ma Ma Hta was what you might call a homing pigeon. She loved to be, and work, at home – finding plenty to do there. Her sisters went out and about with their friends. They liked to travel up to Rangoon or into the Shan States to attend big Christian conventions at which Bible teachers from different countries, including Japan, would preach. If she attended she was always glad to get home.

As regards having a sweetheart and courting in Burma, Ma Ma Hta says: 'When we had a sweetheart we never showed ourselves in front of others. It was a kind of shameful thing to show affection in public. When a schoolboy wrote a love letter to me, I had to take it to Mother; I mustn't reply. When we are older and are in love, unless we let our parents know, the young man can't visit – and we never get together by ourselves. When Hla Thin came down from Mandalay with my brother he was invited in, but I could not go out with him. We all talked together at home! We would never dream of holding hands and kissing in front of the family! In those days we didn't "keep sweethearts". Sometimes when Hla Thin came, we young people walked to the nearby lakes and also picnicked together.'

Now, continuing her letter, Ma Ma Hta may have recalled the day Hla Thin asked her father for her hand in marriage. Both parents had willingly given their consent.

He had soon proposed, whispering that she was 'the only one' for him. He could hardly believe it when she said 'Yes'. But the fact of the matter was that although Ma Ma Hta felt attracted to him physically and enjoyed his amusing company, she was also thinking of him as a desirable sort of person to be linked with, having in mind the social enhancement of her entire family! In Burma there was a consensus of opinion that it was good to make as excellent a match as possible.

Hla Thin was the ideal candidate. He was the eldest son of a much-loved, highly esteemed and well-known Christian pastor. Both his grandfather's and his mother's family had been at the Court of the illustrious King Mindon in the famous Palace at Mandalay.

* * * * *

At last Ma Ma Hta had almost completed her letter. Being 'non-political' she hadn't mentioned politics, although of course she knew that the British who ruled her country, had been at war with Hitler's Germany since September 1939. She had written amusing things about the family which she hoped would make him laugh, and told him what had been going on at the Deaf School in Rangoon, where he had often helped her during the evenings recently.

Theirs had been an unusual engagement, having seen very little of one another. Hla Thin was working hard to provide for his two brothers and his sister financially. In Burma eldest sons were expected to share in financial burdens. The young couple had agreed that they would not be officially engaged until all three had good jobs.

Hla Thin found this waiting almost unbearable. Ma Ma Hta on the other hand, had never been a typical 'girl'.

As Ma Ma Hta finished the letter and addressed the envelope, there was something that she did not know. She had not the least idea of the actual exciting life that Hla Thin was experiencing! There were good reasons why his correspondence lacked news.

At the end of the 1920s, after a Commercial and Business Studies Course in Calcutta, India, he became a stenographer (one of the first batch in Burma). He worked at the High Court in Rangoon for a number of years. In 1938 Ma Ma Hta's elder brother, together with Hla Thin, volunteered to be in the British Army in Burma and were in the crack Burma Rifles Regiment. Then Hla Thin was drafted into the Army Intelligence Corps.

At the time of Ma Ma Hta's writing to him, Hla Thin had the job of working as stenographer with British Army Intelligence officers, more or less living on the stern-wheeled river boats up and down the great Irrawaddy. Hla Thin had inside knowledge of the *Sagaing* area. Political Burmese rebels were organising against the government. There were also illegal small arms dealers, and certain Japanese spies acting as legitimate businessmen but preparing the way for a possible invasion.

Hla Thin, involved in intelligence work during this period and throughout the war, could never give Ma Ma Hta the least hint of either his occupation or his whereabouts!

If only she could have known!

Ma Ma Hta and her Mother after the 1939–1945 war, Rangoon

3

Education and Calling

1941 was coming to an end. Ma Ma Hta was back in Rangoon[1], working in the School for the Deaf.

There were about five certificated teachers and five trainees, with fifty pupils. Most of the children came from other parts of the country and the rest were day scholars from the Rangoon area. All the boarders were from other parts of Burma. It would have been good if there had been more such institutions in the country but as yet there was only the one.

Ma Ma Hta says of the school's beginnings:

'It was opened in the 1920s by Miss Mary Chapman and her friend, Miss Walden, who had already established a similar school in China. They had arrived in Burma in 1919, and bought a big Victorian house in Tank Road. They had begun teaching a small number of children at first, to show parents that *deaf* youngsters could be taught to speak.

'There was no sign-language at that time; only the oral method was used to teach lip-reading and speech. This made the teaching extremely difficult.

'We had a great deal to do at the school. The same staff who taught and cared for the pupils who lived in, took it in

---

[1.] Appendix: Note A: Rangoon City

turns to be on call at night. Life was full routinely, with little deviation from the norm, generally speaking.' But
things were soon to change, drastically[2].

Ma Ma Hta believes that *God* called her to work with the
deaf. She says: 'In 1933 when I was twenty, I wanted to be
in midwifery, having had two years nursing training in
the British Government Hospital at Rangoon. At the same
time I was also interested in the work of the Missions. I
had come up from Kanthonezint with the thought that I
was to begin a midwifery course. I had never heard of the
Deaf School. But our great God moves – he has plans of his
own: man proposes, but God disposes. I went to stay with
my brother Moses' family in Rangoon and one Sunday it
happened that I met a friend of the family named Daw
Saw Tin at church. She asked me, 'Hta Hta, what are you
doing now?' I told her that I was about to join a midwifery
course. Daw Saw Tin mentioned that more *teachers* were
needed at the School for the Deaf, where she gave Burmese language lessons to the missionaries.

'Daw Saw Tin took me to the school the very next day.
By the time I had been shown around, and told the aims of
the school and seen the children, I was hooked! When I
saw them, I fell in love with them!

'Daw Saw Tin was concerned with me, partly because
she was *also* a Mon, one of the ethnic groups within Burma
to be found mainly around the Moulmein area. As she was
talking to me at the school she remarked that there were so
many Christian nurses and asked me why I didn't think of
teaching the deaf. She suggested that I could still do missionary work but with the deaf children. I realised then
that this was my true calling – from God.

'I told the Principal that I would like to teach the deaf
children and joined the school the same day. I began my

---

2. Appendix: Note B: The Governor and Political Change.

training proper in 1934. At first I worked as a student, looking after the children. There was no domestic help; it was very good training for us – we did *everything*!

'The local people would not work with the deaf, as helpers. In our country it is believed that those who are unable to speak are prevented from doing so by certain kinds of evil spirits ('nats' – *narts*) who stop them from saying anything – or else they would tell where the treasures of the gods are. The Burmese also hold the belief that if they come into contact with a deaf person, when they themselves have a baby it will be born deaf.'

The deaf children enjoyed school life. It was made as enjoyable for them as possible. They blossomed and responded well to being treated as normal children. There was plenty of love, fun and laughter for them, as well as discipline and hard work.

As time went by, Ma Ma Hta became recognised and was given the task of travelling to schools in other parts of the country to let people know of the possibilities for those who had the disadvantage of being deaf. Five sensible children went with her. Together with the children, Ma Ma Hta, with her imaginative gifts and lively presentation, would demonstrate how the deaf were being educated. Questions would be answered and in general the Mission School for the deaf came alive to those who listened. The fruits of these efforts were apparent in the gradual increase in the numbers of children entering the only school that could meet their particular needs. They also showed in the amount of money increasingly donated to the establishment by individuals, some of whom had been educated in other Mission Schools and were, by then, heads of big business firms, for example. This type of giving continued for many years. God was giving the increase.

Recently, Ma Ma Hta made the heartfelt comment that she could never understand why the British taught the deaf children to speak in English rather than in their native tongue, which would have enabled them to talk freely at home. Was it because the two English missionaries, having previously spoken in Chinese, were still trying to learn how to speak Burmese?

Ma Ma Hta really understood children. She was full of life, amusing and much loved by the youngsters – especially as she was one of *them* – a national. Their youthful teacher was also an all-rounder, including being naturally good at sports. Those arriving from other Burmese States soon settled down in Rangoon and revelled in being taken for swimming and picnics beside the lake in the park, and being able to see animals in the Zoo and wonderful natural things in the Botanical Gardens. They also looked forward to experiencing camping in the extensive grounds of Government House – by special invitation of the Governor and his Lady. Ma Ma Hta was introduced to him when he came to a Christmas performance given by the children.

* * * * *

Ma Ma Hta says of her own life and education: 'I was born in Bassein on October 30th 1913. My brothers and sisters and I were well disciplined but had a very happy childhood. We had to respect our elders no matter who they were. We would never dream of answering back at any time, even if our elders were in the wrong! We dared not cheek back to any one – even our servants.

'My schooldays were also very happy, though at times it was difficult to be extra good, which was expected of the Headmaster's daughter! I had lots of friends, some younger, some older. I was in a Co-ed School until I reached 7th standard. After that I went to the girls' section of the two schools which had just been built within the same grounds, called The American Baptist Girls' School. Then the competition started! The girls and boys tried to outdo each other in every aspect of life! Having completed 7th standard, I went with my sisters to Rangoon and was proud to attend the Kemmandine Girls' High School, but I was not there for long as I was needed to help mother at home. Later, I went back to a different school in Rangoon till the 10th standard. I got a B Grade in the final exams, and decided to take up nursing.

'General school sports were more or less as in Britain today. In the infants and juniors we played simple playground games like catch, hopscotch, special kinds of skipping, ball games and organised games including racing, as well as having 'drill' (formation exercises, for example, with Indian club-swinging). When older, we played netball, badminton, basketball, tennis, quoits and rounders. Tennis was not so popular with the girls; we preferred badminton and netball. Football was very popular with the boys. We Burmese do, however, have a national game, called Chinlon (*chinlone*). It is usually played by men only, and there are six players. They stand barefooted in a ring. It is played by kicking a special light, cane ball from one player to another without letting it touch the ground, the hand or the arms. You kick the ball with the instep or the right side of the foot. It can be touched with any other part of the body. As you become more adept at it, you can do more trick shots, of course. Chinlon is graceful to watch.'

Ma Ma Hta, being a tomboy, was the only girl who joined in the game locally with her brothers and their friends.

* * * * *

There was yet another intriguing side to Ma Ma Hta's education.[3] She says: 'I want to mention an unusual thing about my schooling in my younger days. I was educated at my father's Mission School, an American Baptist school. (Adoniram Judson was the founder of the

---

[3] Note D: Burma – Education in General

American Baptist Mission and translator of the Bible into Burmese.) When I had completed studies there, my father told me and two of my sisters that he wanted us to join the *Buddhist* School in Bassein for a while, simply because he wanted us to know about how the Buddhists lived and about the religion held by so many Burmese people in the surrounding area. So he contacted the Principal of the Buddhist School and they were very appreciative and happy about that. This was making history – that children of the Headmaster of the Christian School should come to the Buddhist School. Most of the Burmese Buddhist teachers there had been educated at my father's school and we knew nearly all of them. Usually that school closed on their Buddhist day of the week and not on the Christian Sabbath. When we knew we were going to join their school, the Principal asked the staff and the children not to talk about religion; they wanted to show that their religion was better than ours. So we went to the school. When we got there we had to take off our shoes, whether it was dry or wet, whatever! We were there for about a year I think.

'One day, when it was recess (break-time) we went out into the compound as usual, when it wasn't pouring with rain. As I stepped into the classroom after the break, I saw a chalk drawing on the blackboard which showed Jesus Christ on the cross. Everyone was sitting down at their desks ready for the teacher to come in. But I immediately went and stood in front of the class. My sisters and I were the only girls there. I looked at them all, and asked: "Who drew this?" There was no answer. "Haven't you got enough courage to own up?" Still no reply, so I said, "Well, I will tell *you* something. I'm very pleased you have drawn that because I want to tell you about my Lord Jesus Christ, who died for us on the cross – for you all, and ourselves; and he died not for anything wrong that *he* had done, but for love of us all – and he died for our sins." I was also very glad because they didn't know about the Christian life, nor about Jesus; and God had let me tell them about Jesus Christ. From that day on, there was no sign of anything against the Christian life or teasing, or any kind of persecution. I was very pleased. In Burma, to openly confess Christ and to admit to being a Christian also meant that you were not a Buddhist, and people would feel that you were not truly Burmese but pro-British.'

It took great courage to speak up as she did. Maybe her Heavenly Father was preparing her for greater tests in witnessing in the years to come.

* * * * *

'When I was almost fourteen years old, my father wanted me to be baptised, but he wasn't quite sure where I stood spiritually; no one could go through the waters of baptism unless he or she was a truly committed Christian.

'He explained to me that my great-aunt in Moulmein, on the *Buddhist* side of the family, was very fond of me – she thought I was "like one of them" – and she wanted to make me the heir to her considerable fortune, which she could only bequeath to a *Buddhist* member of the family. She had often asked me if I could go to spend a few weeks with her during my school holidays. My father told me that he did not wish to influence me either way, so he said he wanted me to go. I was to make up my own mind as to which way I would follow – Buddhism or Christianity.

'When I got there I found that she had asked two of her elderly, trusted gentlemen friends to give me a few sessions on Buddhist teachings. One man was a judge, and the other an army major. They put me at my ease. "We are here to care for you and look after you. You need have no qualms about that. We have children, and they are very good. We like you too, as a daughter." They began to talk about their religion and spoke of their "lord" (Buddha), in respectful terms.'

The sessions went on for a few weeks. One day they included the words, 'We will find a nice successful young man for you.' This suggestion did not please her. 'I cannot change from one religion to another,' she replied seriously. 'I cannot be bought with money.' They were surprised at her sentiments. She had always been taught to be courteous to the elderly. By way of apology she said, 'I am only a *young* Christian. I don't know what to say.'

'What are you thinking?' asked one of them kindly.

'To climb the ladder is not easy. We have to go step by step,' she answered wisely, and they were satisfied.

In the meanwhile, her great-aunt was doing *her* part to impress dear 'Hta Hta'. She was teaching her the ways and rituals of her religion. Out of deference, Ma Ma Hta felt she must do as her kind aunt required within the house. She changed the daily drinking water and put a bowl of sweet *jagree* before the small shrine and statue, bathed the face and feet of Buddha and nightly lit a candle there. Also, every morning she had to go out early into the streets, to offer alms and food to all the Buddhist monks of many ages in their saffron robes holding their black lacquer bowls. Then she had to *bow down* to them (she had always given them simple respect). These were the rituals she had to perform.

But after all the adults' efforts to change her beliefs, one day the two sincere gentlemen decided to find out where she now stood spiritually.

'Where are you now?' one asked.

'On the first step,' she answered.

'In what way are you thinking?' asked his friend.

'I'm still on the first step,' she replied firmly.

They were exceedingly disappointed.

'It's no good,' they said between themselves. 'We cannot influence her at all. We cannot do anything for her. She's clever. She knows very well.'

Then they addressed her: 'Your faith is too strong in you.

We cannot change you,' they admitted solemnly.

Ma Ma Hta went home to be baptised.

* * * * *

As far as employment was concerned, the current Burmese population in general looked upon it as highly desirable to have a 'good job'. Yet many understood that those who dedicated themselves to the type of work done by religious people, would probably have a different attitude towards remuneration.

The time came when Ma Ma Hta knew that God had called her to work at the Bible Churchman's Missionary Society School for the Deaf. She realised that her pay would be less than if she had done Midwifery. (She had hoped to help support her family). Upon broaching the subject with her father she mentioned that her earnings 'wouldn't amount to much'. He had immediately replied: 'It doesn't matter. I am pleased – that you are to be in the place of *God's* choosing. As long as you are doing *His* work, I am content.'

There had been a time when *he* had experienced comparatively low wages. He had been in a profitable position as a government employee in Rangoon, and had chosen to do what he knew to be God's will – in taking up employment with the American Baptist Mission.

U Chit Htwe came from a family of Buddhist and wealthy landowners; it had not been an easy decision for him to make.

A wedding reception (private) at the Royal Mews, London, 1989

4

The Unexpected

In Rangoon there was a general feeling of prosperity, gracious living, and 'Peace and Safety'.

Even though many people in the city were aware of the advancing gains made by the Japanese forces in southeast Asia, they could not imagine that *Burma* would be over-run because of its strategically difficult terrain. As for the capital – well, they thought it was completely invulnerable! The main Regular Army crack battalions were stationed there; the elected *Burmese* Provisional Government was there; the water, food, money and goods were there. What was more, they believed that they were protected by the bastion of Singapore, where thousands of Allied troops were billeted in readiness for action. Burma's RAF Headquarters was at Singapore. There were also two powerful Royal Navy warships sailing in nearby waters.

* * * * *

23rd December, 1941. What was to fix this particular day in the memories of those at the School for the Deaf – and everyone in and around the city of Rangoon?

Suddenly, into the general noise and bustle of the pleasant town, there was a totally unexpected wail of an air raid siren, blaring out through the sunlit air, then continuing its mournful message – persistently, pitilessly, and inexorably.

When many were taken up with preparations for the
Christian Christmas, which spoke of 'Peace and Goodwill
towards men', such a ghastly interruption was all the
more appalling. But the Japanese had timed their attack
thus.

People immediately panicked, scurrying hither and
thither, snatching up small children, bumping into others,
as they frantically fought to reach a place of safety. As yet
there were no trenches, let alone air raid shelters! Now the
dreaded droning of warplanes was reaching their ears,
then loud explosions in what sounded like the docks area.

In what seemed no time, dozens of enemy aircraft were
already above the eastern outskirts of the city, dropping
their left-over bombs and incendiaries. Then citizens
could hear a more deafening noise following on, as the
invaders were met by Royal Air Force and American Volunteer Group fighter planes. These were soon in combat
with a second huge wave of Japanese military aircraft,
directly above the eastern side of the town. Through
smoke and flames on the ground, people could see and
hear planes zooming terrifyingly as they came plunging
down into the built-up areas.

Then a third wave of about one hundred enemy bombers and Zero fighters roared forward, many of which were
then hit by Allied airmen and the few anti-aircraft batter-
ies in the city.

Before long all was over and the offending warplanes
flew away. The Japanese had managed to discharge most
of their lethal loads onto military targets: the oil refineries
at Syriam, and the Rangoon docks – not intending to
antagonise the Burmese civilians themselves more than
they could help. But the worst scenes of carnage were at
the wharves where hundreds of Burmese and Indian dock
workers were killed. Ships were sunk or ablaze. Ware-
houses were like an inferno.

People in the south-eastern part of the capital could see thick billows of jet-black smoke with tremendous leaping flames coming from the damaged oil installations, rising higher and higher into a surprisingly blue sky.

Needless to say, there was chaos in those affected areas of Rangoon. Ambulances were hindered from progressing through roads littered with debris. Ancient fire-engines were in evidence, but in many streets, water standpipes were not functioning. People were dazedly helping one another as best they could. Some watched their homes burning, while others heard and saw unrecognisable human beings screaming with injuries, slumping in the road before their eyes, many dying – mercifully. Hysteria mounted.

* * * * *

Away to the west of the town (which was not affected), at the School for the Deaf the staff were setting a good example by exhibiting a calm and peaceful spirit.

The *children* hadn't heard a thing!

The railway line, which ran along one side of the school compound, lay untouched by bombs, as was the immediate area. During the raid, one and another of the younger staff had run outside to look at the great number of Allied planes passing overhead and it was a cause of amusement to the children within the building, who were puzzled as to why the staff were behaving so strangely! Nothing was explained to them.

One raid was enough. The missionaries set about arranging for as many local pupils as possible to be escorted home. They were able to telephone some of the parents to collect them. Ma Ma Hta had the job of accompanying individuals or small groups along roads filled with excited people. Some private vehicles, carrying anxious travellers clutching belongings, were wending their way northwards.

She arrived back at the school to find the remaining day scholars and boarders being entertained, very effectively, by some of the staff in the largest, festively decorated room, at one end of which was a lovely Christmas tree. Looking at the happy scene, one wouldn't have dreamt that in the very same town there was destruction and death that day.

After the children had gone to bed the Burmese staff asked the British missionaries of the Deaf School to evacuate the children. They thought it wouldn't be long before the Japanese advanced into Burma. At about the same time, a missionary at the Bible Churchman's Missionary Society headquarters in the extreme north, phoned and offered accommodation to those at the Rangoon school, an offer which was gratefully accepted.

Ma Ma writes:'Miss Chapman said, "Who will go north with the children?" Three of us Burmese teachers put up our hands.'

That same night contingency plans were presumably being made by the Japanese. They had no doubt been shocked to hear that 291 of their planes (including 52 bombers) had not returned to base. This had not been due to any 'suicide' bombing but to the fact that the American Volunteer Group and Royal Air Force pilots had been so successful, in spite of being greatly outnumbered. (The Allies lost 97 planes.)

*   *   *   *   *

It was Christmas Day – 25th December 1941.

Despite the disruptions of the previous couple of days, many Christians had been to their worship services and were on their way to various celebrations afterwards.

But – what was that? Was that really the terrifying drone of another air raid warning?! On this day of all days! How *could* they! Anger took over, as all on foot raced to places of refuge, including any newly constructed trenches which had hastily been prepared by the Government, using hundreds of coolies, after the first attack. But these were only shallow trenches; in low-lying Rangoon, the local water-table was discovered to be too high.

All too soon bombs were falling.

When the raid was over there was cause for rejoicing at Tank Road, for the school and grounds were intact.

The plans for getting away to the north were soon realised. Before leaving, Ma Ma Hta went out to do a little shopping. She was surprised to see that there was no bomb damage at all and that the trams were still running. Once again, the Japanese had aimed at totally destroying the refineries, the docks and military targets.

However, the fact remained that the children were to be evacuated. Ma Ma Hta was thankful to God that the British railway authorities were to give VIP treatment to everyone from the Deaf School on their journey. They would be allowed as much accommodation on the train as they required. Each person was to have a sleeping berth in air-conditioned First Class carriages, which included wash-basin and toilet. Ma Ma Hta says, 'The railway people looked after us very well.'

All British citizens, including missionaries, were ordered to evacuate from Rangoon, and the school was now in the charge of a Burmese Head Teacher, Daw Sein Kyawt, who was to go with the children to the north.

In Ma Ma Hta's words, concerning the last few days in Rangoon: 'Any children still at the school were, in the end, collected by their parents. I volunteered to take those whose homes were slightly further afield, back to their families. Having dealt with those few remaining scholars, I went with two other Burmese teachers and the boarders who were still in our care – girls and a small group of boys – and we evacuated to Mohnyin, travelling on the one train all the way.'

Ma Ma Hta had always lived in the south. Many of her relatives were still in the same area. Family life was very important to her. While she had been working in Rangoon, she had been so glad that she had been able to see her eldest brother, Moses, almost every day.

As the train pulled out of Rangoon station, Ma Ma Hta felt strange, leaving him behind in that potentially dangerous city. She says, 'I was very, very sad at that time.'

Full of prayers for them and for the rest of her family in the south of Kanthonezint and 'committing them into the hands of the Lord', she was hardly able to keep her eyes from brimming with tears in front of the deaf children. Remembering her last telephone call to her old and beloved father when she had sought permission to go north with the deaf children, she couldn't help wondering if they would ever see one another again. Her father always backed her up, considering the Mission work *first*. As the train gathered speed, her fleeting thoughts were, 'If the Japanese attack Burma in force, will they get as far as the Bassein area? Armies usually set up their headquarters in strategically important places... No, I think Kanthonezint and the nearby Burmese and Karen villages are in too much of a backwater.'

Time would tell.

* * * * *

The overland trip to Mohnyin, in Kachin State, was roughly 1,000 miles.

The railway track ran parallel to the main road running north. It became visible now and again to the children, giving them something of interest to watch out for. The train stopped at every station en route, but travelled consistently at a fairly good rate.

Ma Ma Hta comments: 'At all the stations, there seemed to be chaotic activity. Because of the crisis situation, the trains going both ways were overflowing with passengers.' It appeared funny to her that some were travelling north while the rest were heading south. She thought that they might as well have stayed where they were – as far as numbers were concerned! Describing the scenes on the railway platforms – 'The fruit vendors and those that sold other food and drinking water, tea etc. were frantically trying to make sure that all were served before the trains moved off again. People were getting out of the train to get what they wanted, then having a desperate struggle to return to their carriages without dropping anything!'

They had turned eastwards at first; looking out of the train window in that direction, Ma Ma Hta was struck by the great beauty of the distant hills, near the Mons city of Pegu. Then the tremendous gaping mouth of the Sittang river met her eye. At Pegu – which extended over quite a large area – there were modern buildings, superimposed, as it were, upon really ancient ones. The latter, overgrown with ivy and tropical creepers, lent an air of history and intriguing mystery to the town. There was much evidence of the great earthquake in 1931 which had struck the massive Pegu pagoda. Once, the place had been the capital of the kingdom of the Mons people, who had finally been overthrown by the Burmans in about 1066.

Leaving Pegu, the train continued north through the eastern side of the Delta region. The land was like an endless plain. It was covered with paddy fields which were interspersed with clumps of tropical trees, hiding villages. Periodically, Buddhist monastery roofs and spires appeared on the horizon.

The deaf children occasionally saw white egrets enjoying their watery surroundings and colourful, smaller birds or black crows. Where there was flat ground for grazing, there were cattle or goats, but it must have amused them more to see the lumpy, black water buffaloes lazing in the streams or rolling luxuriously in the thick, brown mud.

The powerful engine drew the long train forward, past small shrines, temples and white-washed pagodas. After some time, they came to further rice fields, where at one point the *road* was on a bank six feet above the flooded land – whereon were more herds, egrets and tall, rather morose-looking adjutant birds. As the hours went by, the children inevitably grew bored, although they remained well behaved.

Approaching Central Burma, there were places where the jungle seemed to press in on the train with its wet, steamy foliage reaching forwards in luxuriant growth, and there was little to be seen. The youngsters became restless so the staff did what they could to entertain them.

When the road came into sight again they saw precariously perched passengers, high on the tops of rickety buses, amongst untidy bundles, and baskets of poultry. There were long lines of bullock-carts going through clouds of dust, and also military vehicles, including armoured cars.

At bedtime, all gathered for prayer. Then the great desire to sleep on a top bunk caused jealousies as half the children were allocated to the lower beds!

All had a good sleep. In the morning, as they were having something to eat, they drew nearer to Mandalay. Over to the west, they could see the mighty Irrawaddy – extremely wide and full of vessels, mostly sailing north. The large stern-wheeler boats were impressive. Many were at that time carrying thousands of unfortunate refugees up from the south. The train then stopped at Mandalay where the station appeared to be dangerously overcrowded for a while.

Then they were on their way again, heading towards the Ava Bridge. As they crossed the river, they could see a huge bamboo or log raft, with a lumber-navigator and his family, plus hut, on board. The boys and girls were delighted to see children living on the raft! *Tonkins* – working boats carrying rice – with big, patched sails filling with the wind, were a reminder of days gone by.

Leaving Mandalay far behind and now approaching Sagaing, Ma Ma Hta felt extraordinarily moved, because this was where Hla Thin had spent his childhood.

As they drew into the station, she suddenly saw one of his brothers amongst a sea of faces! He spied her from further along the platform and made his way to her carriage, smiling broadly! He liked 'Hta Hta' very much, and had often thought that Hla had not treated her as well as he should. Once, he had met Hla when he was doing a Course in Calcutta. He had challenged his brother about getting on and marrying Ma Ma Hta. He had wondered why he was taking so long to do it!

She was so pleased that someone had come to meet the train. Ma Ma Hta says: 'His mother had sent him to the station with some home-cooked food for me and the others, with a message of warning as to what we should or should not eat at the station, due to the prevalence of disease. It wasn't even safe to take a bath in the river!' She immediately passed on the news to the staff in case anyone was thinking of buying food.

As soon as she could, she found out from Hla's brother that her fiancé was still in India as far as the family knew at that time. None of them had seen him for what seemed ages. Ma Ma Hta felt greatly relieved that at least he was out of danger.

* * * * *

By the time they reached the Mission Headquarters at Mohnyin, the three adults were ready for the welcoming cup of tea. Despite feeling strange in their completely new surroundings, the youngsters were raring to go! They became slightly less bewildered as they experienced a loving reception and a familiar type of meal. They were then shown to the Chapel building, where they were to camp for the rest of their stay. The main mission house had already been filled with yet other refugees.

Ma Ma Hta ended the day with a very thankful heart and as she drifted off to sleep, she was vaguely aware of the cooler temperature in the hills of Upper Burma and enjoyed the warmth of the embers of the log fire, which was in an enamel wash-basin on the Chapel floor.

Hla Thin, on the other hand, though only the other side of the nearby Indian border and, as the crow flies, not so very far from his love, had heard of the bombings of Rangoon and was worried about her. He longed to be with her once more.

5

War on Mandalay

In Mohnyin – high up in the health-giving atmosphere of the Kachin Hills – the work of teaching the deaf children was continuing peacefully. The Burmese staff were encouraged by the progress of their charges; with only twenty of them and being able to devote more time to each one, they were becoming far more confident and their speech was improving dramatically. Also, the teachers themselves were learning better ways of helping to make educational subjects more easily understood. There was plenty of time for practical demonstrations by both pupils and adults – through miming, for instance.

One day, Ma Ma Hta had a surprise. Her brother, Moses, and his wife arrived from Rangoon and were put up at the Mission. It was good to have one of the family there.

It was during the long evenings and at night, that Ma Ma Hta was free to think more about her family and Hla Thin. She remembered those days in Rangoon, when she had visited Moses at the YMCA. It was at that Hostel that she had first seen Hla Thin at one of the nightly Prayer Meetings. He and his brother, who shared a room with him, used to come to her brother's family maisonette. As time went by, Hla Thin had taken many opportunities to visit the Deaf School to see her, even when it was her turn to look after the children, and he would help her to keep them all happy. 'He was very good with them. He used to tease them and make them laugh. They were fond of him.'

One night, Ma Ma Hta lay thinking that it was strange that she had never met his mother. Now that she was in the north, she wasn't so far from Sagaing (about 200 miles). It would be lovely to go and see her, and to see the rest of the family again, having met the others in Rangoon. But it was out of the question to take a trip by herself to Sagaing at that time.

During the night hours, she used to think of her fiancé's life as the son of a Baptist Pastor. He had been brought up in that family of four boys and one girl, used to the rough and tumble of existence with brothers. He had also become accustomed to discipline, as his father had expected his offspring to set an example in their daily lives. They hadn't found it at all easy! Ma Ma Hta had realised that because he was a naturally more quiet and observant sort of person, he gave the impression of being dignified – even in his youth. It was probably due to the fact that being the eldest, it had been beholden upon him to act responsibly. But she had seen another side of him: he could be full of fun and very amusing in company, especially when with children.

Initially, after seeing him several times at the YMCA in company with other young men at Moses' place, Ma Ma Hta had found that she disliked him! She thought he was argumentative, particularly during discussions. She also considered him selfish! Maybe this was partly because his mother thought that he rarely put a foot wrong! Nevertheless, she had soon realised that he was attracted to her, as he was 'always watching' her!

One springtime night, lying awake on the chapel floorboards, Ma Ma Hta recalled the time when her fiancé had first told her now much he cared for her but she had continued to regard him as an attractive friend. (In Burma, special respect was paid to the sons of religious people – like Pastors and *Hpongyis*, meaning monks; that was another reason why she had accepted his attentions graciously.) Their friendship had gone on like this for quite some time. When he had first begun coming to the Deaf School of an evening, she had been more concerned that the missionaries might not approve of it. But they allowed it. By then, he was deeply in love with her. To be near her, he offered his help with the children, saying 'It's just being with you, and *seeing* you – that's enough for me.'

When Hla Thin had asked her to marry him, she still had not fallen in love with him but saw it as a special privilege to receive such an offer because, as she explains: 'I gave respect to all the families of the Reverends.' It was also from that point of view that she took the big step of accepting. But she had not remained unmoved by his tender profession of love.

In thinking back over Hla Thin's past, Ma Ma Hta was aware that she had come to appreciate her fiancé more and more, for himself. Also, she thought of his many talents – especially on the arts side. He could write poetry and short stories, some of which had been published: one had been read on Radio BBC Rangoon. He was quite good at painting, and was also musical, preferring the classics and playing both piano and violin, and singing in chapel choirs. He also liked modern 'swing' but not jazz, enjoying the wartime songs already in vogue – such as 'The White Cliffs of Dover' and buying records to play on the gramophone, as well as the music scores of classical or recent works.

Ma Ma Hta herself had a really poor opinion of her own educational attainments. She thought her sisters were cleverer than she was, and were much better at speaking English correctly. She felt that Hla Thin was very well educated. His parents had been enabled to give their off-spring every opportunity to realise their potential.

Hla Thin's mother was cultured, having grown up in Court circles as the daughter of one of the ministers of King Mindon (and for a short while, of his son, when he had become last King of Burma). Hla's father U Law La, had met and married Daw Thin, who was *also* descended from wealthy land-owning stock. Later they had both been converted to Christ from Buddhism. Daw Thin's parents were staunch Buddhists and they had disowned her. However, she had been quite content to live simply, as a Pastor's wife and a mother, not only to her own children, but to everyone with whom she came into contact.

During the night hours, Ma Ma Hta sometimes had disquieting thoughts about possible dangers that might assail her loving fiancé – after all, it was wartime and he was in the army. But then she would pray for him, and sleep in peace.

* * * * *

The famous town of Mandalay was *also* 200 miles from Mohnyin.

Ma Ma Hta explained why she had to take a trip to the city, in April 1942 – and what took her there:

'In February, all the British were ordered by the UK Government to leave Burma. So our Principal and BCMS missionaries had to evacuate too. Our Principal left a cheque to cover our salaries and other expenses. It was some time before we needed cash. We had gone without our salaries while at Mohnyin, but in the end it was necessary to cash the cheque, which could only be done in Mandalay. Our Burmese Senior Teacher was not happy about going so I volunteered.'

In the end, she was accompanied by Moses and his newly married second wife, and the younger Burmese teacher. None of them knew whether the Japanese had reached Upper Burma by that time. Ma Ma Hta committed them all into the hands of her all-knowing Heavenly Father, and they set out.

As they walked the few miles downhill towards Mohnyin station with the beautiful scenery all about them, there was not a soul to be seen anywhere – which was unusual. She couldn't help feeling a little vulnerable, though she had never been the type of person to panic.

It was very quiet, except for the twittering of a few birds and the call of a kitehawk. It would have been good to have seen some of the local Kachins. Their women were fresh-complexioned, black-haired, and graceful, always walking upright. They invariably wore hand-embroidered, handwoven wrap-around skirts over dark, fitting trousers, black close-fitted jackets sewn in splashes of brightly coloured silks, if they could afford it, and the adult women had a band of woven material round their heads. Their waists were bound with a broad sash and they wore sandals.

The proudly erect men were usually in dark, loose trousers, open-necked shirts, straight loose jackets of a lighter hue, sandals or shoes (if worn). They had a neatly tied band of cloth on their heads, finishing in a tuft at one side.

In his book *The Land and People of Burma*, C. Maxwell-Lefroy of the Burmah Oil Company, who gave a copy of his book personally to Ma Ma Hta, wrote '... young men, sturdy and smiling, for Kachins are a breed of soldiers, like the Gurkhas ... Kachins have to work desperately hard to scratch a living from the mountainous, jungly country ... Their villages are usually perched up on top of steep hills ... In these remote parts, you never quite know who your enemies are!'

According to Charles Nicholl in *Borderlines*, there were a 'lot of jade mountains controlled by tribal rebels'. The jade was 'some of the finest in the world'. The Kachin men

carried long swords in metal scabbards, which were hung
from the left shoulder.

* * * * *

It was 3rd April 1942 – Eastertime – and it happened to be
what the Christians call Good Friday. In other years, Ma
Ma Hta would have spent part of the day at a chapel, hearing the preaching, praying, and meditating upon the his-
torical day on which Jesus Christ had died. But everything
had changed for her.

At the station, a freight train arrived and the four travellers clambered into a dusty goods wagon. The three
women were wearing the usual dress of the Southern Burmese – flowered cotton longyis and a blouse – their hair
neatly done up in a 'bun', and Shan cotton shopping bags
slung over one shoulder. Ma Ma Hta, always ready for
emergencies, had filled hers with a First Aid kit and a
small pillow into which she had stuffed some money.

There were a few silent passengers within the railway
wagon, very few travelling at all during that time – 'only
evacuees, probably'. They settled themselves with their
backs against one splintered side of the truck, also preferring to maintain silence. Ma Ma Hta reflected on many
things and of course spent part of the long journey in
prayer, just talking to her Father in Heaven. She also
thought of Mandalay, that she had visited once, years
before. She didn't really like the town, which she had seen
'with its shimmering heat, dirt, open drains'. She preferred the countryside around Mandalay 'with its trees
and orchards – lovely!' The town had many very old, picturesque Burmese buildings, constructed mostly of wood.
The British had added their own even more durable struc-
tures. The most important Burmese architectural work,
just outside Mandalay, was the massive 'fort', surrounding the remains of King Mindon's famed wooden Palace.
The British, renaming it Fort Dufferin, were using it as a

military base, having insensitively filled the huge grounds of the Palace with barracks, parade grounds, an arsenal and sporting facilities, such as squash and tennis courts, and football pitches. Ma Ma Hta had been driven past the huge walls of the Fort, once; it was an impressive sight, with its unusual ornate towers – typically Burmese. She wasn't interested in seeing the inside of it, at any time.

Mandalay – to the Buddhists – was a centre of Burmese culture, to which they looked as to a mother. At the foot of Mandalay Hill was Kuthodaw pagoda, in which were huge slabs of carved Buddhist texts, commissioned by King Mindon, in 1862 (according to the writer, Mr Waitt, in his book *Sights*).

* * * * *

Ma Ma Hta and the others would have been very disturbed if they had known that the Japanese had indeed invaded Burma[1] – and occupied Rangoon, on March 9th. More so, if they had known that some of the enemy forces had entered eastern Burma from Siam, had outflanked the British Forces along the border and were heading straight for Mandalay! What was even worse, the main strength of the British Army in Burma, then under General Alexander, was being forced to withdraw all the way along the banks of the Irrawaddy and was making a last stand in a ferocious battle on a tributary, in Upper Burma, called the Pinchaung – not far from the city to which Ma Ma Hta was going! Also, she and her friends were unaware that about 100,000 refugees from the south, who had come up by road, rail or river, were by then southwest of Mandalay, awaiting transport to take them towards the western border so that they might escape into India. There were already cases of cholera. A trickle of more fortunate ones had begun their long trek to the border mountains, where

---

[1] Note C: The Invasion

the Governor had made sure that dumps of food, blankets etc. had been placed along the main Tamu track. Through the Governor's foresight, outside Mandalay had also been prepared, with food, and facilities such as First Aid, with preventive inoculations etc. and sanitation but these were in the event insufficient for the enormous numbers fleeing from the Japanese. Many would soon be flown to India – including the Governor's wife and daughter – but the vast majority would have to trek out.

Ma Ma Hta, blissfully ignorant of the situation, approached the city from the north-west, crossing the steel-girder Ava Bridge over the wide river – the only one on the whole of the extremely wide Irrawaddy – and the four travellers arrived safely in the untroubled town. There were several British and Chinese soldiers walking about the streets, the latter being part of Generalissimo Chaing-Kai Shek's (Allied) Forces, who were under American Lt General 'Joe' Stilwell's Command.

Ma Ma Hta and company proceeded towards the house of one of Moses' personal friends, a Burmese Mons Army officer and his wife, who were Christians. They all had some distance to go. Passing through the attractive older side of Mandalay, with its jumbled wooden homes, they stopped to shop in Zeygo market, near the old Victorian Jubilee clock tower. After the cooler climate of the Kachin hills, they felt that the city was like a furnace; it was an extremely hot day. Ma Ma Hta kept on remembering that it was Good Friday – normally an *extra* special day for her.

The banks were all closed because of the British and Burmese Christians' Easter weekend. They were therefore unable to obtain any Kyats (*chetts* = banknotes in ones, 5s, 10s and 15s) that day. They continued on till they reached the Burmese officer's fine-looking timber home, built upon thick, wooden stilts, where they were welcomed with surprise. The husband was away. There was also a young Burmese teacher and another lady there.

Ma Ma Hta had hardly set foot inside when there was that spine-chilling wail of an air raid siren! All were immediately precipitated into alarmed action, as the sound of enemy planes from Siam and the people shouting and screaming outside in the street, resounded in their ears. Then bombs began to fall.

'In the house, we were all terrified, and began running here and there to find a hiding place. We separated, and didn't know who was where. No time to think. Advice received in Rangoon passed through my mind, that during a raid, we were to go into trenches or any air raid shelter, protect our heads, and lie flat. I ran to the kitchen and made my way towards the back entrance. Suddenly, there was a terrific explosion which blew the door in! Momentarily shocked, I turned away and happened to see a wash-basin, which I grabbed, and raced through the side door and down the outside steps to hide under the house with the bowl on my head, lying face down on the dusty earth.'

The bombs were incendiaries. Fires had started, particularly in one area of the town. Dry-timbered Mandalay was horribly aflame.

Ma Ma Hta had not been told that there was a communal, recently dug trench in the back garden. The lady of the house did not yet know about the trench because she herself had come up that day from Rangoon. When the raid was over, Ma Ma Hta realised that 'going to hide beneath the house was a fortunate move, because the next-door neighbours who had taken shelter in the trench, had all been killed instantly, with a direct hit! It was wonderful how God spared *me*: I knew there must be some purpose in it! Was it because of the deaf children? Or my people? Or my parents?

'After the bombing, I ran up into the house, and was so overjoyed to see everyone safe and unharmed. I realised that there was no time, because of the fires, and urged them to hurry and pack all the mosquito nets, medicines and First Aid kits and their money.' Decidedly practical, she rushed to the bedrooms and hastily tore down the army mosquito netting from above the beds. Then with arms full she walked towards the front door agitatedly, wondering why there was so much delay in vacating the house. Her friend was trying to collect jewellery and valuables. Ma Ma Hta suggested that it was more important to remain *alive*, than to worry about those things; medicines to prevent them from getting malaria were much more important at such a moment.

'It was not in fact very long before we got out of the place, where we could see that the whole city seemed to be an inferno with great flames leaping high; the extra heat was unbearable. We quickly piled everything into Moses' friend's car, and headed off towards the south-western suburbs, making for the American Baptist Mission's Girls' School compound.'

The short journey was like a nightmare; where houses had caught fire, timbers were falling at odd angles into the roads, people were running hither and thither in panic regardless of traffic, streets were blocked and there were ghastly sights, never to be eradicated from the memory. War is despicable. Those citizens who were still alive were supporting the wounded or carrying the dead and making their tortuous way to Mandalay Hill, on the east side of the town, not knowing that that was the very quarter from which the Japanese hordes would, ere long, run into Mandalay! Yet other suffering people were toiling towards any nearest exit that would lead out of the city.

Two-thirds of Mandalay was burnt.

Ma Ma Hta says: 'When we arrived at the ABM compound, there were crowds of other Christians who were
from all directions. Some were refugees, just arrived
before the bombing, who were from Rangoon; teachers
from the Blind School were there, who had also come up
north with *their* pupils.'

(It happened that Ma Ma Hta's father – once a 'staunch
Buddhist', as was her mother, 'who slammed the door in the
missionary's face' – were both converted to Christ through
the preaching of the American Baptists in Moulmein). Ma
Ma Hta says: 'These Americans in Mandalay did not turn us
away, but when we saw the overcrowded conditions, we
thought it better to move on. One lady in our party was able
to phone someone she knew and was going to be picked
up by car and remain in the suburban locality, whereas I
was driven by car away from Mandalay that evening and
crossed over the Ava Bridge (soon to be blown up by the
British so that the Japanese would be hindered from pursu-
ing both the refugees and the army to the Indian border). We
travelled about 200 miles in a state of shock – into the peaceful region of Sagaing.

'I did not know what had happened to Moses and my
new sister-in-law. We had become separated. Some people at the Mission who were driving to Sagaing offered me
a lift. As for me, I decided to go to my *fiancé's home* for a
while, before going back up to Mohnyin.'

* * * * *

Strange to relate, it so happened that the writer, Leslie
Glass, was also passing through Mandalay on 3rd April
1942. He arrived there after the raid. The fires had taken
their toll. In commenting on the dreadful scenes of death
and destruction that met his eyes, he wrote of a further
impression made on his senses and his mind:

'... the acrid smoke of smouldering buildings and
remains of trees. One (tree) stood like a black cross against

the sky.' He writes that that particular sight caused him to remember that the day was – Good Friday.

(Good Friday is so called because it is Good News day – remembered in the Christian calendar – when Jesus Christ was nailed to a 'tree', and died for the sins of the world.)

6

Sagaing to Bassein

Sagaing was unforgettably beautiful, set amongst parallel necklaces of low-lying hills which were positioned on lovely, fertile, narrow strips of plain. The hills were wooded, with some of the 'slopes covered in frangipani, bougainvillea, tamarind and mango trees' (Klein Wilhelm: *Burma* – Insight Guides).

The entire area had an ethereal atmosphere. It was of special significance to the Buddhists who regarded it as sacrosanct. The Governor of Burma had recently given his word to the people that there would be no military action whatever, within the region. (Lt General W. Slim, Commander of Burcorps, would not be aware of this until he had set up his Army Headquarters there in May, the following month!) The HQ was promptly transferred.

'In the vicinity of the (Maha Aungmyne Bonzan) monastery is the Adoniram Judson[1] Memorial' (K. Wilhelm).

* * * * *

Ma Ma Hta was making her way the following morning to the Baptist Minister's house – Hla Thin's home. (She had stayed the night with the people who had driven her to Sagaing.)

[1.] Note M: Adoniram Judson

Out of the many thoughts troubling her, after all the
evil events of the day before, one was to remain with her
for many years: 'The Japanese always seem to bomb on
our special Christian Days. They did the same thing in
Rangoon – on Christmas Day.'

She was looking forward to being with Hla Thin's parents. By now she felt physically and emotionally drained,
she was hungry and thirsty and her clothes were slightly
soiled due to lying on the earth under the house. She
hadn't thought of tidying herself up; there were far greater
matters assaulting her mind, which she was turning into
prayer.

Ma Ma Hta says now: 'Then came the high spot – amidst
the shock of the previous day's carnage and mayhem.'

At last she was walking up the pathway towards the
'Vicarage'. She had a lovely welcome from Daw Thin –
and Hla Thin himself! All three were amazed!

Hla Thin was almost overcome with delight when
he set eyes on Ma Ma Hta! What a reunion! So much time
had elapsed since they had last seen one another. How
wonderful of the Lord to arrange things in this way!

When comparing notes on what they had both done on
Good Friday, they were surprised that they had both been
in Mandalay on the same day! Hla Thin had arrived in
Burma on a secret mission, with express orders to destroy
all money that was left in the Maymyo Army Base Headquarters. He had flown over the India-Burma border with
some British officers, landing at Meiktila, one of the few
airports. From there he had gone up to Mandalay, expecting to continue on to Maymyo, only to find that the Japanese were already there. The other officers probably went
to the Army Base in Fort Dufferin, and he was free to go
home for the day. Hla Thin had also expected to 'sort out
the Army pay' for his unit in India at a Mandalay Bank but
the Japanese happened to raid the city.

So both Ma Ma Hta and Hla Thin had been in Mandalay hoping to obtain wages for staff! Neither of them was able to go to a bank during that week to get any money at all.

As all the family gathered around her, Daw Thin was glad to become acquainted with her future daughter-in-law. Their hearts were full of praise to their loving Lord. Later, as they sat over a meal talking, their joy was tinged with grief when they realised more fully what had happened in Mandalay.

Hla Thin had bad news for Ma Ma Hta, revealing that the Japanese had taken Rangoon and seemed to be advancing rather than being defeated. He could not tell her all that he knew. He said that he could only stay for a few hours, as he was expected back in the Mandalay area overnight. He hoped to see her the next day if practicable, but his personal activities were limited.

As it turned out, it was a whole week before he was to say a final goodbye. It so happened that during the times that he came and went each day, Ma Ma Hta and he were hardly able to be together alone for more than a few *minutes*. We can imagine their shredded inmost thoughts and feelings.

At the end of the week, Captain Hla Thin's orders were to join the rest of the Burma Rifles Regiment, at Shwebo, prior to being flown back into India. General Alexander's headquarters were at Shwebo. Because of critical circumstances, only he and Lt General Stilwell had been able to meet there, where they decided that there was 'no choice' but to order the entire British Army to evacuate from Burma.

* * * * *

Whilst Hla Thin and Ma Ma Hta said their fond goodbyes, they were loath to part, so very soon after meeting again. But now they were both aware that their love was strong.

It would stand the test of any vicissitudes of war and separation.

Since then, Ma Ma Hta has confided: 'Our love for each other was a pure love. It did not need the external trappings of what some people call "love" today.'

In an understatement she has written: 'It was nice to see him unexpectedly in Sagaing. It was really a bonus!'

* * * * *

After leaving Ma Ma Hta and his family, Capt Thin managed to board a passenger train. It took him as far as Shwebo. There the remnants of the much-depleted British forces were also collecting to await further orders. That train had been the last one to go south. It had only gone a few miles when it was bombed and derailed, blocking the Mandalay-Rangoon track for at least a month.

Hla Thin was offered a seat on what was thought to be the last flight out of India but noticing a frail old Indian woman and her young companion, he was given permission to let them both travel in his place. He knew that it meant trekking – out of his own land.[2]

* * * * *

It was a whole month before Ma Ma Hta was able to return to Mohnyin. The trains were running again. Hla Thin's uncle, and one of his brothers, accompanied her to Sagaing Station, then travelled one stop with her to see her safely on her way. There she was, in a railway truck with bare boards, alone for the rest of the journey. She wanted to be with the children again.

'Instead, my folks from Rangoon were waiting for me at Mohnyin and they told me about my school group being taken by the Burmese teachers further up into the mountains to a village called Nawku, where some Kachin Christians had offered them all hospitality and care.' Ma Ma

---

[2.] Note E: The Trek

Hta was extremely upset that the children had been moved without her; she felt responsible for them. It was not possible for her to get to Nawku.

'On the other hand, it was an unexpected pleasure for me to see Moses and his wife again and now to see my two younger sisters – one with her eight-month-old baby, Babs; plus her Indian Nanny; and my other recently married youngest sister, who had been living in Rangoon. Both sisters had come north to fly out to India, where their husbands were, but had missed the planes. They wanted to trek out of Burma. It was a mercy that they were prevented from going on that hazardous trek.

'I was happy to know that my school group was in good hands with the Kachin Church Elders. I was glad because I then realised that I was at the right place, at the right time.'

There were to be further tests yet for Ma Ma Hta. Although the deaf pupils had been taken out of her hands, she was being strengthened spiritually for greater responsibilities ahead.

* * * * *

Ma Ma Hta's sisters had been accompanied by an Australian jockey from the south, and two young men from Rangoon known to the family, who came with them to the Mission House in Mohnyin.

By May 20th, the Japanese held most of Burma.[3]

The Imperial Army announced to the population that free transport was to be laid on so that anyone could return to their homes in safety. They said that there was no need to fear – Burma was now independent from the British. A Japanese soldier came to the Mission to give the refugees this news.

The whole party decided to leave the north for Rangoon, but Ma Ma Hta had not been back in Mohnyin very

---

[3.] Note F: Burmese Attitudes

long, when suddenly malaria struck the group. The middle-aged Australian had a very bad bout of it. As usual, it fell to Ma Ma Hta to do all the nursing, both day and night. She only managed to snatch a little sleep now and then.

Their plans had to be changed. It now seemed better that Ma Ma Hta should take them down as far as Sagaing to begin with. She was feeling disappointed, as she was so looking forward to seeing her father and mother, but the jockey was too weak to undergo a single lengthy journey. Also, he was in doubt about whether to go south at all. He couldn't make up his mind what to do. He wanted to go to India.

As it transpired, in spite of painstaking nursing care, he was obviously failing physically. He died. Ma Ma Hta says: 'We gave him a simple burial service. He was laid in the grounds of the Mission at Mohnyin. Everyone was very sad and shocked .... We arranged to write a special letter to his home when postal services were back to normal.'

Shortly after the funeral, the group left Mohnyin. Ma Ma Hta says: 'I managed to get them, all nine, down to Sagaing. Once again, I was at the right place at the right time, and said the right things to the Japanese at Mohnyin Station so that I was given a whole railway carriage for my family, our two friends and myself. But we all managed to get down to Sagaing by the grace of God.

'Unfortunately, we lost our Nanny, Naimi, after we arrived there (due to malaria). It was a great loss to us. I wondered if there was a purpose – I realised at the time that HE spared *me*. I praised the Lord.'

Hla Thin's family squeezed them all in, some at the Baptist Mission House and some at the Vicarage. The youngest sister was pregnant and unwell. None of them expected to be there long.

They had to stay in Sagaing until August!

'We had not been able to continue our journey to Rangoon, because now my brother, his wife and Barbara's (Babs) mother were all down with malaria. Only my youngest sister and I did not have it.'

By then, Ma Ma Hta was very tired.

'I was so frustrated! All I wanted to do was to get back home to my parents and the rest of my family in Bassein. Instead, I was held up longer than ever because I had to look after the sick – all by myself!'

* * * * *

'By the beginning of August (1942), the health of the two who were still suffering from the effects of malaria improved sufficiently for us to act upon the Japanese Government's offer of free transport.'

They all travelled by passenger train to Mandalay, then were to be changed onto a goods train which was to go non-stop from there to Rangoon.

There was a terrible crush of people at Mandalay Station. Ma Ma Hta was taking the Nanny's place virtually, and was holding the baby. At first she was somewhere at the back of the queue at the platform barrier. A few Japanese soldiers were trying, without much success, to control the crowd, saying sternly to individuals and groups, 'Stand here!' 'Wait there!' and slapping people when they were not obeyed. Ma Ma Hta had an opportunity to step forward, and nobody stopped her. In fact, as she walked a little further towards the platform they were making way for her and the child. She found that she could continue going towards the train without any trouble! She was able to get in and reserve some spaces in a goods truck, beckoning to the others to join her, which they did after a while. 'It was as if a way was made for us to go forward. Whether it was a miracle or not, I don't know. The Lord had given the responsibility to me.'

The party was finding the truck hot and overcrowded, without any facilities. Ma Ma Hta's sister was feeling sick. The only positive thing that could be said about it was that the journey was quicker than it would have been if there had been a normal train service.

They all arrived at 2 a.m. in Rangoon, hungry and exhausted. As they were walking out of the station, Moses (Scout Commissioner and well known in Rangoon), who was with them, happened to come across a particular young man who had been one of his Scouts, who owned a 'trishaw' (tricycle with two-seater cart). On hearing what Moses was about to do, he immediately offered his vehicle to him, if it would be of any help. 'Then he went off to buy us some tea and cakes from a stall, at his own expense, for which we were more than ready. He next proceeded to load our luggage onto his trishaw. The rest of the baggage was given to three or four coolies.

'He said he knew where we could go for the night, and led us to St Gabriel's Church Hall, which he told us was a haven for refugees. It was very crowded, but as it was the early hours, we stayed there until the morning. Our heavenly Father cared for us.

'The next day we hired one *chaigary* (two-wheeled hardcart) and a small *gary* (horse-drawn carriage) – for those who were too weak to walk. We went to our old friend's house; she used to be Matron of the Christian Hospital. She willingly accommodated us and did everything she could to make us comfortable. I thought we would only be with her for a few days, but it happened that we were there for about a month, as my youngest sister was really ill. She was expecting her first child and was still very weak now through malaria.

'As soon as possible, I rushed out and made my way towards the Rangoon river, to see if I could book a cabin on a ferry that would take us to Bassein. There seemed little hope of accomplishing this, as there were hundreds of other refugees seeking to do likewise.

'My mind was so full of anxieties about getting my pregnant sister home before anything should happen to the unborn baby that I had rushed out of the house without thinking of putting on my shoes. I ran hither and thither through the streets towards the river where the ferry-boat to Bassein usually came in. The strange thing was that there were no Japanese soldiers to be seen anywhere. They must have known that the people would not try to give any trouble, as they had advised us not to be afraid.

'At last I was at the docks, where a few Japanese soldiers were keeping in order the many refugees. Suddenly a man approached me and spoke to me. He was one of Moses' friends! "What are you doing down here?" he asked, in some surprise.'

Ma Ma Hta was so glad to see someone she knew, and soon explained her situation.

'And what are *you* doing now?' she queried, certainly not expecting the answer that he was to give!

'I'm helping to run the river steamers,' he replied. She could hardly believe her ears! 'Three of our party are still down with malaria. I must have a berth for them.'

'Yes, all right,' he said simply.

Her troubles were almost over. Thanking him happily, she hastened back to tell them all. She was conscious that the Lord himself had 'gone before'. They really were in his wonderful care.

Ma Ma Hta says: 'We moved to another friend's house to be nearer to the jetty. We were there a week, waiting for the boat.'

When the ferry came, there were hundreds of refugees struggling to get aboard with a few Japanese soldiers to control them.

'That night the ladies and Babs were in a cabin, and I slept on deck.' If they had gone along the coast of the delta, they would have been at their home port within twelve hours, but the vessel wound its way through the smaller tributaries, which took much longer. All of them must have been longing for the journey to come to an end.

The previously bustling port of Bassein was comparatively quiet now, as they docked, at about 7 a.m. Then they had to wait about another hour before disembarking. There were no Japanese to be seen. They hired two motorbikes with sidecars, with Burmese drivers, and a bullock cart for Moses and his wife plus luggage. Ma Ma Hta herself used a trishaw as they all made their way slowly out of the town, where there *were* a few Japanese soldiers – which must have sent a pang into her heart – as she hoped desperately that her family at Kanthonezint were unharmed.

Ma Ma Hta's father and mother and the two younger brothers were there to greet them. Moses, their eldest son, had come home as well, so now it was like a real family reunion – all except for the one who was with the British Army in India. 'All hugged each other!'

7

Japanese Occupation

The home-comers found themselves in the same old Kanthonezint but there was a difference. The Japanese were in the area. Some of the people they knew had left the village.

Ma Ma Hta was struck by the change in atmosphere among the local people. They were not happy. Most of them were 'very much afraid of the Japanese'. They were no longer free. Many men and youths had been rounded up to do the work of labourers, day after day.

They were pleased and encouraged to see Ma Ma Hta again. Many had known her for years. They were very glad to have her back, 'partly because I was like a quack doctor or nurse! We – that is, our family – had been looking after local people's health and helping them financially. If necessary, we had taken them to hospital.' She had been saddened to see that her parents seemed to be much weaker now – especially her mother. Also, that her two younger brothers appeared to be overstrained.

The incoming party was told that the Japanese had ordered that everyone must learn the Japanese language and go to the classes but none of the adults in Ma Ma Hta's family attended. 'I did not like the Japanese. I did not recognise their rule. I did not want to learn their language.' One of her friends had learnt the language quickly and taught the local children. People had begun to speak Japanese when necessary.

One morning, a Japanese officer came to see Ma Ma Hta's father, U Chit Htwe. He was invited in. Upon entering, he respectfully bowed to the old man, knowing that he had been a reputable Headmaster in Bassein. Despite this courtesy Ma Ma Hta felt uneasy. She could hardly wait to hear what the officer was going to say to him. What did he want? She thought that the Japanese were not to be trusted. She had heard several bad things about them. She was exceptionally protective of her much-loved father. Without a doubt, she was ready to fight for him to the last.

'There is no Headman in this area of Kanthonezint,' the officer stated. 'I have come to say that we wish to appoint you to be the Headman.' He finished lamely, his dead-pan facial expression revealing nothing of his personal feelings in the matter.

The young woman immediately feared for her father's well-being if he was given such a task. Several thoughts flashed through her mind: 'It would be too much for him, overtax his strength and make him really ill – and I've heard that the Japanese have a habit of publicly slapping the faces of any man who annoys them!'

Her emotions suddenly welled up within her. She couldn't bear the thought of one of them touching, hurting or humiliating him. She was certain that she would never forgive the man who slapped him. In a highly emotional state by now, she said to herself: 'If they do slap him – it doesn't matter whether they kill me or not – I will do something to *them*!'

Ma Ma Hta says now: 'That was in my heart. So I just told them that he was too frail and old. I spoke out to them and said, "When you are not satisfied with my father, you will slap him – that's what I am afraid of." So I just asked him, "Can you make *me* Headwoman in his place? I could do his jobs for him. If you can, please do me that favour".'

U Chit Htwe sat there, amazed at his daughter's spirit. It had been a risky thing to do. (Ma Ma Hta says now, that her mother did not agree with the idea at all. She kept shaking her head and saying 'No, no, no'. 'My father and I didn't like her doing that.')

There were about 200 Headmen in the south-western Bassein area at the time.

The upshot of the request was that the Japanese appointed Ma Ma Hta to be the Headwoman of Kanthonezint, in charge of about 200 families. We believe that she was the only Headwoman in Burma during the Japanese occupation.

* * * * *

At the beginning of her time as Headwoman, Ma Ma Hta prayed earnestly that her Heavenly Father would enable her to do the job. She did not doubt that it was he who had allowed her to be appointed. She says: 'God gave me a special word from the Bible to rest on at that time. It was the verse that says, "I will give you a mouth and wisdom!"' (Luke 21:15).

In her position, she was able to appoint an assistant – a young married man called Maung Ohn Shwe (Maung means younger). His sister, who lived with the couple, was about to have her first baby. They lived in a house opposite Ma Ma Hta's.

The neighbours and the people in the village across the main road were surprised and delighted to hear the latest news about Ma Ma Hta, whom they all knew well. Her own mother had reservations! After all, she knew her better than anyone, except her husband, and realised that her 'Hta Hta' could be impetuous at times, and on occasions had spoken out far too frankly! Under the circumstances, she may have been worried about these particular traits in her daughter's character. Her father, on the other hand, trusted the Lord implicitly, and knew that what he had begun in a person, he was able to perform. He knew that she wasn't perfect, but he believed that God was leading in Ma Ma Hta's life.

It was the special work of the Japanese *Kempetai* (Military Police) to look out for dissenters to the Japanese will. The aim was to control minds. Everyone was ordered to attend Japanese language classes for a start. Also, because of their fear of possible pro-British spies in their midst, they arrested and questioned a few unfortunates. This served to intimidate many Burmese who 'did not like the Japs'. They were too terrified to defy them. The vast majority simply acccepted what they were expected to do, day by day, as do many peoples living in war-torn countries.

Not so the Headwoman and her family! They ignored the language lessons yet were never reprehended.

Although the military conquerors had already commandeered a few of the finer local houses, they were still in need of accommodation. One day, Ma Ma Hta was told by one of the Japanese that Mg Ohn Shwe's house was required. She was very cross. 'No, they cannot have it,' she said. 'That man's sister is almost in labour. She cannot be moved at this time. This is the only house for her: there is nowhere else for her to go.'

'Please do not talk to him like that,' warned the young Burmese lad who was acting as interpreter.

'The officer is talking to me – not to you,' answered the Headwoman.

Ma Ma Hta hesitated for a moment – then the words *'Honjo kikan'* came into her head out of the blue. She had once heard a Japanese officer saying something like that and had noticed that when the words were pronounced, the soldiers present had looked nervous and had fallen over themselves to do what they were told! So she said the magic words:

'You had better go and ask *Honjo kikan* if you are allowed to take this house.'

Immediately, there was an entirely different atmosphere and the officer to whom she was speaking changed his mind and stopped the soldiers from taking the property!

Up until this time, the Japanese had been taking houses at will. Strong teak homes had been occupied within a very short space of time. Of the four Christian Karen families, only two remained. Some people had left the area voluntarily when hundreds of troops had arrived at Bassein and the Japanese 55th Division had set up their Headquarters in the district.

There was a small monastery next door to Ma Ma Hta's home – a short distance away. One monk was in residence. He was 'like a sort of Bishop'. The monk was afraid of the Japanese, according to Ma Ma Hta, and he now made up his mind to leave Kanthonezint. He approached the Headwoman and asked her to keep an eye on the monastery buildings while he was absent. So Ma Ma Hta had charge of the Buddhist Monastery! But the Japanese soon chose to commandeer it to be the Health Officer's and Supply Officer's quarters. Also, a few soldiers lived in it, who assisted with the preparation and distribution of goods to the local army units. The building was fairly small, with two storeys. There was also room for military patients when needing treatment from the Health Officer.

Before the *Hponji* (monk) went, Ma Ma Hta had stored some of their best family furniture in the monastery, for safety's sake – in case they had to evacuate. There were, among other things, a marble table, a marble dressing-table, and their beautiful mahogany dining table. (We shall see later what took place with regard to the latter.)

* * * * *

Without wishing to overload this book with too much military detail, it does seem necessary to clarify the situation in which Ma Ma Hta was expected to work as Headwoman during a war.

At the enemy's General Headquarters there must have been consternation. Their supreme object had been to make a super-assault on British India as soon as was practicable. Burma was in a chaotic state in some areas, with criminals etc. taking full advantage of the situation. Internal evacuees had mostly returned to their own localities, but there was a great shortage of administrative staff for the country districts. The British had held most of the Civil Service posts, assisted by mainly Burmese subordinates who had been well trained, worked extremely hard and who, in accompanying the officers in their ICS (Indian Civil Service) duties, had gained a certain amount of 'know-how'.

As time went by, encouraged by the Japanese, a number of the Burmese subordinates returned to their old jobs in the rural areas and in towns, and they became officers for the first time. The busy Japanese left them to get on with their occupations and gradually these Burmese-appointed subordinates were making quite a good job of what they found to do in spite of the almost impossible state of the country. However, there were many Burmese who had worked in administration with the British, who did not trust their masters and would not go back to work – for the enemy.

The country was in a state of flux. News travelled slowly. The invaders had stolen nearly all personal fountain-pens and radios. Telephone systems needed repair. Couriers had to go great distances. If the people had not proved docile, governing would have been even more difficult.

The Japanese Command realised that they must try not to be seen as a threat but as a friend, in contrast to the colonialist British. The populace must trust them and settle down so that the Japanese could finalise the deployment of their forces for the major assault.[1] The problem was how soon they could achieve this. Given enough time, the British could strengthen their Indian defences, and maybe make a powerful move to re-enter Burma.

The Japanese were making sure that there were trustworthy Headmen who were capable of keeping the country-folk quiescent. All these things were done for the greater glory of Japan and in line with her strategic ambitions throughout the East.

* * * * *

Ma Ma Hta was a Headwoman, yes, but she held this position in perspective. She says: 'There were already about 200 Headmen in the south-west Bassein area. They were *real* Headmen, who had held their positions since before the war.' Most were elders who had been approved by their local people.

Obviously, things had changed a great deal since the departure of the British. Ma Ma Hta did not have to do many of the duties normally associated with village Headmen in peacetime. For instance, she didn't have to wait for the regular visits of an ICS officer. He used to come to check on crops, drainage, possible diseased cattle and general upkeep of the land and paths etc. He would have looked at the Headman's register of births and deaths, records of the number and kind of vaccinations and inoculations, and cases of serious human illness such as virulent tropical diseases. He would also have found out about any strangers who had passed through. Ma Ma Hta would never have to make a plea for government aid

---

[1] Note G: Burma's Wartime Provisional Government

– for the repairing of roads, small bridges, strengthening of the river-banks, minor dams or anything like that, help in land revenue problems or for extensive damage of crops. (Leslie Glass wrote: It was 'A fair system humanely and impartially applied'.)

As Headwoman under a different management altogether, the young woman had no idea from day to day what would be required of her and there were many fierce tests ahead. She says of this period: 'I worked extremely hard. I had strength. I was never afraid of the Japanese. I tried to show that our family was a *Christian* family – always, under any circumstance.' Of course, she puts this resilience down to the constant ability given to her by God himself. 'My family and I always worked *together* – being Christian. My father always trusted and believed me.' She found herself in difficult and sometimes dangerous situations. 'At the time, most people had a very rough time – men, women and even children.' Her own family was comparatively well treated, partly because her father had been a headmaster and they respected his daughter because they knew that she was a teacher of the deaf – but it wasn't long before she was suspected of being a spy.

Ma Ma Hta had been giving nursing help when she had first come home, and still endeavoured to get to the Bassein Hospital to help out whenever she could, but she found that all kinds of incidents kept cropping up regarding the local Japanese platoon, and she was responsible for seeing that justice was done in cases where the villagers were directly affected. The lower ranks would sometimes 'go wild' – and come into the villages to get possessions, or chickens, ducks etc. They would bully the women when the men were all away working, and 'the people were so frightened that they would just let them take anything'. Someone would then run and call the Headwoman and she would have to face the soldiers fearlessly, and ask them why they were doing it without permission. She said to a couple of them one day – 'If you do it, I will report you to *Honjo kikan*.' They had not understood all her words, but when they heard '*Honjo kikan*', that was enough for them and those two were never seen locally again! Ma Ma Hta thought that *Honjo kikan* probably had something to do with a powerful Military Police officer at the local army administrative office.

There were other days when the young Japanese troops ran into the villages and caused havoc, terrifying people, stealing what they fancied and then running off quickly, which meant that in those cases the Headwoman was unable to help sort things out.

* * * * *

One afternoon, Ma Ma Hta was walking back from the hospital. There were houses straggling along both sides of the road. She was almost at Kanthonezint when she heard the sound of one of the usual platoons of soldiers jogging behind her – as they were doing their usual daily exercises. She stepped onto a low mound at the side of the roadway to give them room to pass and as she did so, one of the young men playfully gave her a slap on the backside, much to the amusement of those with him. Then, of course, he jogged on.

But he hadn't reckoned with *this* particular Burmese woman! He had no idea what a mistake he had made.

Ma Ma Hta got down off the mound and ran to catch up with the offender. Naturally, she wasn't going to have any Japanese soldier treat *any* Burmese woman in such an extremely insulting manner. She would see that he be taught a lesson that he would never forget! She jogged beside him until the soldiers were lining up in ranks before their sergeant. He had seen her and sent a soldier to escort the Headwoman to himself – mightily surprised to see her jogging in with the men!

(One of the ladies who lived in Bassein and had known Ma Ma Hta since she was a child, happened to look out of her window and saw her jogging along with the platoon. She told her afterwards that she had thought to herself, 'What is that dare-devil doing now?!')

Ma Ma Hta had only gone along with the men because she thought that she would not be able to identify the offender when she reported him later – as all the 'Japs' looked the same to her!

Ma Ma Hta stood before the sergeant, in front of the whole squad. At first, he waited for her to speak. Then he asked, 'Why are you here?'

So that all could understand what she was saying in reply, she hit on the idea of miming at the same time. This attractive Burmese woman half turned – then pointed towards the Nippon soldier and hit herself on her back. The sergeant got the message and immediately became furious. He moved towards the men and pointed to each one in turn. When he came to the guilty man, Ma Ma Hta nodded, and said, 'Yes'.

The sergeant ordered him out to the front, and at once 'gave him a resounding smacking – on both cheeks'. Then, much to his astonishment, the sergeant heard the young woman call out 'Stop! – that's enough'. He saw her raised hand; then he stopped the punishment and barked out the order, 'Go back!' to the hapless man who marched back into the line in the most profound shame. Due notice was taken of this by all males present.

All the men watched the Headwoman walking towards the offender, talking to him quietly for a few moments. The soldier did not understand what she was saying, but he could tell by her loving tone that she was being kind to him. In fact, she was talking to him as if to a young lad and telling him to think about it and amend his ways. Then, turning to the sergeant, she said: 'That is all.

Thank you,' and walked away from the parade ground, everyone watching her go, in silence.

Several lessons must have been learned that day!

'I knew that it was God's working. He shut the mouths of the lions – so to speak. I, a Burmese woman, was able to make my point to the fearsome Japanese. I came away freely.'

* * * * *

One day, as Ma Ma Hta went to do her nursing, she stepped out of the extreme heat into the slightly cooler Bassein Hospital wards, and received a shock. She was passing by the screened-off private 'rooms', which were reserved for certain patients. In glancing around one of the screens she was surprised to see two American airmen! The hospital was normally used for the general population. The Japanese had commandeered schools and set up their own army medical units for their military wounded and sick.

She walked into the small room and questioned the airmen. One of them seemed to be delirious and she found his speech incomprehensible. She soon learnt from the other that their USAAF plane had been flying fast and very low over the Bassein area when it had been caught by anti-aircraft flak and had crashed not far from the town. The Allies had recently resumed their bombing of specific military targets in Burma since their retreat into India.

While changing both the Americans' medical dressings, Ma Ma Hta was horrified to see the true physical state of the young men. The older one, who was about 25 years of age, had a terrible gaping wound. One arm had been severed from his body. The other airman, not more than 18, had a horrid head wound, with blood still seeping down his face onto already-dried blood. Unfortunately, there were only two or three nurses plus Ma Ma Hta and just one doctor to deal with all the patients in the fairly

large hospital and that included surgical cases. The other
medical staff had evacuated. As she had been expected to
come in to work that day, these two men who had been
attended to upon admittance, had been left unattended
since, whilst awaiting her arrival.

The older American introduced himself to the young
Burmese woman as 'Ed' and his buddy as 'Jack'. She in
turn said, 'And you can call me Ma Ma Hta – Ma Ma
means sister,' she explained. He was glad that she could
speak English. As she changed the dressings that the
doctor had first put on, Ed proceeded to tell her how they
had received their wounds. She, presuming that he
would say that they were due to the crash, could hardly
believe her ears when she heard the real reason for them.
The Japanese *soldiers* had perpetrated both serious injuries. She could hardly bear to listen as he went on to say
that his young buddy, Jack, had been hit very forcibly on
the head with a rifle butt and he, according to Ma Ma Hta,
'had gone crazy'. She had wondered why his wandering
speech had been unintelligible. Feeling desperately sad
that such a tragedy should happen to a fine young man,
she continued listening to Ed's explanations. He was telling her sorrowfully that when the plane hit the ground
the other six crewmen had been killed, yet all that was
wrong with him was that he had a broken hand. The
troops who found them watched while one of them got
an axe and hacked off his whole arm. (Apparently there
had been no officers present.) No medical aid had been
administered. The airmen had been taken along to the
general hospital.

Ma Ma Hta knew enough about nursing to see that
though Ed's wound had been washed and disinfected
upon arrival, unfortunately gangrene had set in. She
thought that the septicaemia had probably been caused by
the unhygienic axe. In such a tropical region this could so

easily happen within a very short space of time. Penicillin was not as yet in general use.

During the following days, she saw one or two local Japanese officers pass through the hospital but no special medical help seemed to have been requested for the Allied prisoners. (The general philosophy of the Japanese militia was to despise all prisoners – as they were thought to be a disgrace to their own nation. They also applied this to themselves.) The visiting Japanese officers probably took note of the Kanthonezint Headwoman when she was caring for the Americans. They already suspected her of being a spy. She began to be cautious about the amount of time she spent with the two patients.

'At one point, Jack was going to be moved out of the ward, but Ed told them firmly that they were to leave him where he was. He always protected and saw to the needs of Jack very well.'

One day, Ed asked – 'Ma Ma Hta, do you mind if I call you sister? I feel you *are* my sister.' She said, 'No, of course I don't mind.' She was pleased that he wanted to call her by that name.

Another time, he asked, 'Sister, can you get me some scent, or some talcum powder? I can't stand the smell from my wound.' She said that she would bring something that smelt nice.

Ma Ma Hta says: 'If it had been a wounded *Japanese* soldier who had asked for scent – I would have done the same for him.'

The weather was steamily hot. Ed had a temperature that would not go down: he was constantly thirsty. As she was leaving the room, he asked, 'And can you bring me some tea? I would love a drink of tea.' She got the Indian hospital cook to make him some. Both men drank the tea. As she went home, she wondered how long both of them would last out. Jack also had septicaemia. She wanted so

much to make their final hours as bearable as possible:
there was nothing else that could be done for them.

When she next saw Ed, she handed him her only bottle
of Yardley's English Lavender Water, which was now
unobtainable in Burma. It was the one scent that she ever
used. There was also a box of powder. He was delighted
and used them on himself straight away – then, beaming,
enjoyed the beautiful perfume that filled the room. The
other odour had made him feel ill.

In one of the short periods when his 'sister' appeared to
nurse both of them, he shared one of the things that was on
his mind. He said, 'Supposing I go back home to my
sweetheart – will she still love me – without my arm?'

'Of course – if it is true love. That won't matter. If it were
me, I would think that this happened to you because of
your good, loyal service to your country. She will be very
proud of you!'

'I feel so happy now, because of what you've said,' Ed
told her, and he felt peaceful about the whole situation.
She found it difficult to look him in the eye – as she knew
he was sure to die.

Ed may have felt that his new sister was no less than a
sort of ministering angel. The day came when, as she was
tending his wound she said, quietly, 'Don't worry about
anything. Just trust in God.' After a pause, she added, 'I
will pray for you.'

'Are you a Christian?' he asked, with some surprise. He
had presumed that she was a Buddhist, in this Buddhist
country. Ma Ma Hta talked with him for a while about
that.

Young Jack was receiving the same amount of attention
as his counterpart. The gentle Burmese woman would sit
by his bedside, changing his dressings and feeding him.
There were no indications that he could appreciate her
kindness. (She says now, 'I felt at the time that I was going

through the same thing as they were – just like them'.) One day, she said to Jack, 'Don't worry. I know that God will look after you. I am praying for you.'

Ma Ma Hta had been really careful not to be seen too much with the Americans. She was glad that one of the local Karen doctors from the town had taken to looking after them in the evenings.

Suddenly, one day at home, she received a short message: Don't come any more to the hospital, because the Japanese know that you are helping the airmen. She realised that she would be arrested if she showed her face there again. The warning had come through one of the *Japanese* officers who had told the Karen headmaster of a Bassein Christian school. It was U Charles Taw, who had been her headmaster at the Powkaren High School for a short while and knew her family.

Ma Ma Hta says: 'The Japanese used to get Charles Taw and me to do various jobs for them.'

She managed to find out what was happening to the Americans. Mercifully, Jack died peacefully, being taken out of his misery.

One night, Ma Ma Hta had a dream about Ed. She dreamt that they were taking him away from the hospital, but the dream did not reveal where it was. Later, she was told that the Japanese had moved him. She still has the feeling that he died on the way. He had been extremely weak when she had last seen him.

She was sorry that she had never been able to say 'goodbye' to either of them.

Major Hla Thin and Ma Ma Hta, Margate, 1970s

8

Tribulations

In August 1942, the Japanese had appointed U Ba Maw to be Head of the Executive. In November, two members of the Provisional Government of Burma walked to India to procure aid for the embryonic Resistance Movement against the Japanese.

Far away, in the suburbs of Bassein, the Burmese people knew nothing of these affairs, of course. They were taken up with surviving in their changed lifestyle, under their eastern masters – realising that, although they had been told that Burma was already 'independent', they had no choice but to do whatever they were ordered to do. They knew that the war was still on and that the British and Americans were increasing their air attacks (some crews flying three or four sorties a day). Periodically, they could hear bombs dropping somewhere in the Bassein area. Fortunately, none had fallen on Kanthonezint. It was military targets that the Allies were after.

The Japanese officers had taken to wearing mufti – possibly to blend in with the population – particularly as a low-flying reconnaissance plane had been seen. Ma Ma Hta had also changed her gear. She had decided to wear men's clothes. She donned a man's hat, Shan trousers which were wide, and a man's coat and shoes. She also carried a man's umbrella when it rained. She thought that

would ease matters when she was among some of the
Japanese. 'One or two did get the wrong idea', she says.

Ma Ma Hta's mother was suffering with her nerves. It
certainly did not help her to hear the sounds of air raids.[1]
Neither did it help the frail, elderly lady when her Hta Hta
was having to do so much for the invaders, and one could
not know what a day would bring forth for her dear
daughter, or indeed for any of them. She had never been in
such a weak state, and it did not help at all when the Japanese took it into their heads to begin to *torture* some of the
local people whom they knew, in the next door monastery.
The sessions took place in the middle of the night.

Her husband and daughter became seriously concerned for her: she was showing signs of real depres-
sion. They discussed the possibility of moving slightly
further away from that concentrated military area to a
peaceful backwater across the river, called Thudawgon
village. Ma Ma Hta felt that it wouldn't be too far for her
to travel into work in Kanthonezint from there. The fact
was that something had to be done very soon to help her
mother.

*   *   *   *   *

As previously mentioned, the only well in Kanthonezint
with pure, spring drinking water was in the compound of
U Chit Htwe. The family had built the compound fence so
that it curved in towards the house around one side of the
well – so that anyone coming along the road could use it.
As in so many countries, wells become meeting-places,
where local gossip and news is passed around. Their well
was no exception, but even this relaxing habit was often
curtailed because one never knew when a soldier would
hear them and they would have to break up the party by
his appearance on the scene. Most people's lives were

[1.] Note H: Allied Military Efforts: 1943

more solemn then, and the Burmese felt it deeply as they were great ones for a bit of fun.

In connection with the well – one day the Headwoman was asked by an officer if she would provide eight Japanese airmen with food and drink whenever they presented themselves at her house. She was already supplying the militia with a lot of foodstuffs from the garden, but now they gave her a fairly large field in which to grow vegetables. They also provided her with two Indian gardeners. She was thankful for that. When the Japanese had first descended on the area, some of them had just walked into people's compounds and taken whatever they wanted to eat, but Ma Ma Hta had gone out to tell them that she didn't like them coming and taking what didn't belong to them! She had said, 'Ask and I will give you, but you must ask *me* if you want anything – not just take it.' So after that, even the officers asked her for what was required! It was a risk she took, but it was part of God's blessing that there was always sufficient food in the garden for the family to survive, though of course they were eating only half the amount that they had consumed in the days before the war.

The eight Japanese airmen for whom Ma Ma Hta had to cater, were seen one day, walking towards the well. Ma Ma Hta was horrified to see that the young men were clad in nothing but G-strings, and carried only towels. They obviously hoped to have a wash-down.

Ma Ma Hta lost no time in hurrying out to them, calling out, 'No! – No!' – then with repeated shakings of her head, and pointing to their state of undress and then to their towels – she mimed putting one around herself to cover her body. Then pointing to herself, said: 'Woman Headwoman not like you coming without cover. Go back!' The men, who had no idea of the sensitive feelings of the Burmese womenfolk, were bemused at the

Headwoman's attack and turned round to jog away to their quarters. Some time later they appeared again, all suitably attired – in their underwear. They saw the Headwoman waiting for them and were surprised to see that she was smiling, clapping her hands, showing her approval, and saying the Burmese words 'Very good!'(Ma Ma Hta says now: 'Because of the strictness they respected me very much'.)

Next day, she went to those in charge and complained at the unseemly behaviour of the airmen, in order to explain that the Burmese women expect respect from the men: they certainly could not tolerate such goings on. Presumably the aircrew were reprimanded and were thereafter on their best behaviour at all times – especially when they came to receive prescribed food rations at the hands of the strict Headwoman!

The Japanese officers were probably making an effort to placate the Burmese women; they didn't want to exacerbate the situation, so they let them have some leeway – without of course injuring their own discipline. Their on-going policy included avoiding unnecessary antagonisms.

Surprisingly, sometimes the officers took to informing the Headwoman as to exactly when the airmen would be coming next, after flying in from their sorties. This meant that she had time to tell her women helpers from the village to prepare the rice by pounding it, and to pick the fruit etc. She did not take part in the preparation of the food, but gave orders such as: 'I want four cups (a pint) of unpolished brown rice, large tins of fresh milk, enough eggs and vegetables, and two hands of bananas.'

Gradually, the officers depended on Ma Ma Hta more and more. They regarded her as very efficient and they realised that it was quicker to ask her to see that a thing was done than to waste time explaining to other individuals. She always found the officers very polite but some of them expected too much of her. Also, the women were finding themselves unable to get a regular good night's sleep because they were called upon to serve extremely late meals whenever new officers passed through the Bassein environs, presumably going on to defend the *Arakan* region,[2] which was being attacked by the British. The Japanese were receiving massive reinforcements by sea at that time, from Java, Malaya, Siam and some of the Pacific Islands which they were losing to the Americans.

* * * * *

While Ma Ma Hta had been up north in Mohnyin, the Japanese had taken U Ba Tun, one of the respected Karen Civil Service officers, for interrogation and *torture*. He had been appointed during the days of the British Administration. The family knew that he was completely innocent of spying. The Japanese could get nothing out of him. After that they took his house, and he and his relations had to move. Subsequently, other innocent people were rounded up, questioned, and then had excruciating pain inflicted upon them.

The torture sessions invariably began between 1 and 2 a.m. One of the preferred methods of extorting information was by beating, and if that didn't work, gallons of water were poured down the unfortunates' throats, then their stomachs were pressed as more water was poured in, which resulted in some of them actually drowning.

Spine-chilling cries would issue from the torture chamber, which was so near to Ma Ma Hta's house – strong pleas, such as 'Help! – Mercy, Master! – Mercy!' and 'Master! No! No! I'm going to tell you! I will tell you the truth!' There were repeated ghastly shrieks and soul-searing

---

[2.] Note I: British versus Japanese: 1943

moans. There were cringing, terrified cries of 'Master, I'm afraid!' and 'Please don't! Please don't!', accompanied by shouts and screams.

Ma Ma Hta's mother heard everything as she lay awake hour after hour. Her daughter couldn't sleep either, and was losing her appetite.

It was during that period of torturing, which took place night after night for at least a month, that one of the high-ranking Japanese officers – in fact Honjo himself – was talking to Ma Ma Hta one day. (He had asked her for Burmese words on other occasions.) It was a macabre conversation, the horror of which she would not fully understand until some time afterwards.

He was talking casually to the Headwoman about Burmese words again; then followed it up by asking, 'Now what is the Burmese word for this?' – pointing to one of his fingernails. Of course, she told him that the word for it was *letthair* – not suspecting anything.

'And what is the Burmese word for these?' he asked innocently, pointing to his calf; then toenails and knees. Having received the information required, he calmly went about his duties.

Ma Ma Hta was told later that the Japanese had begun to extract torture-victims' nails, one by one – they also beat their calves until it was impossible for them to remain upright. Ma Ma Hta was haunted for some time by the fact that she had, albeit inadvertently, in some way helped the torturers to inflict further wounds on her people. U Chit Htwe's entire household went through a more gruesome time than many of their neighbours.

Ma Ma Hta's mother now took a turn for the worse. She began to sit motionless during the day – staring ahead of her for quite long periods. The rest of those in the house went about their normal business, and were kept busy by Ma Ma Hta. Baby Babs, who was now one year old, was a picture of health, with large, twinkling brown eyes and a mass of shining back curls: she brought a great deal of joy and amusement into their lives. They all adored her – especially the grandparents and Ma Ma Hta.

On account of everyone's welfare and safety, it was decided that it was time to move, when practicable, to Thudawgon village.

Of course, the Headwoman had to let the Japanese know of their intentions. They were not pleased with the idea; it might interfere with the smooth running of the immediate area. So far it had been comparatively easy for them to have a strong Headwoman on hand if there was any problem with the Burmese people. They were strict with Ma Ma Hta, and suspicious, too, saying that there was no need for *her* to move, even if the family did. However, she stood her ground, because her parents were old and unwell, and the last thing she wanted was to leave them unattended.

Then the officers made it hard for her to live elsewhere, politely telling her that she would have to report at their office at 7 a.m. daily! They realised that she was not going to change her mind, and did not order her to do so, but arranged that she should work until 2 p.m. each day and said that they would still require her help, and her brother's, at night whenever they needed her to be on duty, as had happened hitherto. ('Gradually they wanted me, and not my brother, but I said "Not without my brother!"')

Ma Ma Hta was determined to let them see that she was a good Christian, no matter what they put in her way. She would be the best that it was possible to be.

Her mother was by now 'very, very depressed'.

The minds of the whole family seemed to be under attack. At such times, it was good to remember that as Christians they were not wrestling 'against flesh and blood, but against principalities, against powers, against the rulers of the darkness of this world, against spiritual wickedness in high places'. They could 'withstand in the evil day' (Ephesians 6). Had not the Lord Jesus 'spoiled principalities and powers' already! They could triumph – in adversity – and be more than conquerors through him who loved them.

* * * * *

By September 1943 the arrangements for moving to Thudawgon had all been made. They wanted to move well before Christmas. Moses and his second wife were about to return to Rangoon.

Burma, being a tropical country, was a place where seasonal diseases took their toll – especially in the Southern Delta region. Many families had lost members including children through illness. Babies could be taken with dysentery, which was a fairly common malady. The horribly damp monsoons brought on bronchial troubles. The major diseases were tuberculosis, plague, chronic amoebic dysentery – and of course malaria.

Suddenly, young Babs was struck down with malaria. In Mohnyin she had missed it when most of them had it. The family didn't care about the delayed move – they only wanted the child to recover. She was almost two years old and so far had been healthy and strong. She looked so pathetic lying there in her little cot, with a high fever. Everyone took turns in nursing her except Moses. Most Burmese adults knew exactly what to do when it came to malaria: it was so prevalent.

After some hours, when there was no sign of improvement in the child, Ma Ma Hta was thinking of asking for their elderly Indian family doctor, Dr San C. Paw, to come over. He lived nearby, but it was during the night. Dr San C. Paw was the most experienced, the most trusted, and best loved physician in the whole of the Bassein district. He was 'just like a father to the town'.

Ma Ma Hta was taking no chances. She could bear the suspense no longer and sent a message saying that Babs was 'really very sick'. Between the time that the person had delivered the message and the arrival of the doctor, Ma Ma Hta saw Babs turn blue and go into convulsions with violent muscular spasms.

Dr San C. Paw hurried to see the young patient; he was very fond of the child. As he stepped into the house, Ma Ma Hta saw that he had no medicines – no black bag. She took him straight to the toddler then stood quietly by while he assessed her condition. There seemed to be a long silence, then the old man said solemnly, 'Either she will die – or, if she does survive – she is likely to be deaf.'

Deaf? The word echoed hollowly. Ma Ma Hta's mind went numb. Deaf – of all things. He turned back to look at Babs again for a few moments, at the end of which he proffered a ray of hope:

'There is one cure that has been known to be successful in a few cases.' He looked at the familiar face of Ma Ma Hta – now care-worn – and said to her: 'If you get ice-cold water, and drop a drop a minute upon the crown of her head – doing it for quite a long time – it could cause the fever to go down.'

Ma Ma Hta thanked him from the depths of her heart, as he departed into the darkness of the wartime blackout. Extremely weary by then, as she had undertaken the longest vigils day and night, she went quickly through to the kitchen. Lifting up one of the large earthenware pitchers of cold drinking water from the cool tiled floor, she poured some out. She ran upstairs to get a pipette. She was soon holding Babs in a sitting position and dropping the drops as recommended by the physician. The family was in the room. The atmosphere was tense. Many prayers were being said for the little one.

After a long time they still could not see any change in
that small body. Ma Ma Hta meanwhile had been thinking. She remembered that when she had last been in Rangoon, she had bought a few medicines off the traders on
the pavements. From an Indian she had procured a very
small bottle of something which was said to be a cure for
malaria. She thought that she must try it. One of the other
women in the house sat by Babs, while she went to get the
bottle. The label cautioned an administration of only one
drop to be taken with water. She was afraid of experiment-
ing with it on a child. However there seemed nothing else
to do. It looked as though Babs wouldn't survive the night
hours anyway.

When Ma Ma Hta returned to her, she was lying inert.
She thought she might be dying. Ma Ma Hta tried to keep
her hands from shaking as she filled a teaspoon with
drinking water then added a single globule of the potion.
She held a blob of cotton wool, pressed it into the spoon
and then wiped it between the child's parted lips. As some
of the medicine went into her mouth, they all saw her
move then heard her say 'Mmm!' But after that she lay
still.

Ma Ma Hta's heart was too full. She suddenly left the
cot and went upstairs with the medicine. She knew what
she had to do. She took her Bible, put it on her divan bed
and knelt down beside it to pray. She opened the book
before her at random but did not read it. First, she prayed,
'O Lord – I am the daughter of my father, and my parents
have so many children. All except my younger brother
"Baba" and me, have their own children. I am the only girl
left unmarried. Barbara (Babs) is my sick sister's first and
only child. Father and mother have always loved and
adored her – all of us do. I too love her very much – from
the very beginning ...' she owned, heartbrokenly, with
tears pouring down her cheeks. 'O God, please hear my

prayer. Take my life instead of hers. I am the one who has no husband and no children – so it doesn't matter so much.' (She felt that in spite of Hla Thin it would be all right. He could find a good partner.) She continued, 'There are all the grandchildren who are alive and well, with my people – and they will be with my father.' She cried out, 'Take my life. I will give my life for hers.'

Ma Ma Hta then looked at the open Bible. It happened to have fallen open at the page in the book of 2 Kings, chapter 20 where the text was about King Hezekiah of Israel 'being sick unto death'. The King did not want to die and pleaded tearfully with God. The prophet Isaiah came to him with a message from the Lord, to tell him that he would heal him: 'I have heard thy prayer. I have seen thy tears ... I will add unto thy days fifteen years ...'

Ma Ma Hta says: 'So I just closed the Bible – and went running down the stairs to my people, who were gathered in the downstairs room. As I went down I was speaking ecstatically, in faith, saying joyfully, 'She is not going to die! God won't take her! She is going to live!' Moses, my eldest brother, was at the foot of the stairs. He thought I had hysteria – so he stepped forwards and gave me a resounding slap on the face – thinking to calm me down.'

Ma Ma Hta says now, 'I was so angry! He hadn't done anything at all for the child! He hadn't shown her any love – nothing. I looked at him with blazing eyes and said, "*You* think I don't know what I'm doing! Do you know what *you* are doing? – you yourself! At night do *you* pray for her, care for her? Do you do anything for her?" He could not answer. Probably overwrought, and with a certain amount of righteous anger, I went on, "I am the one who has been seeing to her needs night and day. It was me that the doctor told to drop the water on her head for hours. I was the one who got the Indian medicine and took the risk with the child to see if it would work – I have borne most of the stress. I am certainly far from being hysterical! And what have *you* done?!"'

Ma Ma Hta commenting recently on this particular incident said, 'I really was a big mouth that time! I thank God he healed and spared Babs. The rest of the family said that it was "a real cure", "It's a miracle!" –but not Moses.'

There was great jubilation in the U Chit Htwe house that night. The crisis was over. God did indeed heal Babs, and spared her life, for more than one purpose – as we shall see.

Babs never had another bout of malaria. Most people do have recurring malarial attacks through the years, once the germ has entered the body.

Ma Ma Hta lives with her today – in AD 2000.

9

Thudawgon

'At last we moved across the river to the Burmese-named *Thudawgon* village – in about November 1943.' The family had told some of their Burmese friends in Bassein of their plan to go and live beside one of the Karen villages, which they already called *Thudawlu*. The Karens had agreed to them building on adjacent land. Prior to their move, Ma Ma Hta, her brothers and some Burmese friends, helped in the construction of their own simply designed Burmese longhouse and then began a large church hall, that U Chit Htwe wanted.

Their move was planned initially by her father and executed mostly by Ma Ma Hta herself, assisted by her younger brothers. It took a week to transfer every necessary item – bedding, clothing, 'Singer' treadle sewing machine, tools, kitchenware, food and, finally, each member of the family. They were to use homemade bamboo mats for sitting and sleeping on.

Ma Ma Hta was healthy and strong although much thinner. She and her brothers had loaded objects onto their bullock cart, driven it to the Bassein tidal river where they had a moored sampan, into which they had fitted a few articles on each trip, then slowly toiled in rowing across the wide waterway to the entrance to a long, winding creek. Thudawgon was roughly two miles further along the creek. Thus they transported most necessities to their new home.

At last the day came to move the family. By nightfall they were all enjoying their first evening in new surroundings. The atmosphere was fresher, as they were on a low-lying hill surrounded by trees and fields and could feel cooler sea breezes.

A few Burmese people from Bassein had preceded them. Before long, the family were joined by their friends from the same town: mainly Christian teachers and their families that they had known for years.

In the community there was a glorious and peculiar feeling of freedom – simply because there were no Japanese to be seen!

But their sense of earthly freedom was shortlived. One day a sole Japanese soldier marched into Thudawgon. At first he walked about, observing everything and everyone. Then he stopped at a certain corner in the village and made a show of stamping to attention on one chosen spot, which happened to be opposite the frontage of U Chit Htwe's house.

The family would become accustomed to seeing the young man on that stamping ground, day after day. They would also get used to the fact that every one of them was watched daily, and saw notes being jotted down on paper, whether it was in the early morning, the heat of noon, or late into the night. (He slept in a little hut that he made.) They called him 'The Watcher'. There was no doubt that he executed his duty in an exemplary manner.

Occasionally U Chit Htwe would have a word with him: the man knew a little English. The 'elder' probably presumed that all the adults in the family were suspected of being involved in espionage! He knew that in Burma the Japanese felt a certain amount of insecurity and suspected every Burmese of being a potential traitor to their cause.

* * * * *

Two years had elapsed since the first bombing of Rangoon. Thousands upon thousands of enemy soldiers had overrun most of the country, with mostly trickles of reinforcements to follow. But there were still a few tracts of Burma, mainly in the extreme north, left unpenetrated. The Japanese were now concentrating on preparing their forces for an attack on British India – which they had high hopes of gaining for Emperor Hirohito of Japan.

Now began a long period of intense pressure for the Headwoman of Kanthonezint. The officers gave her even more work to do. The Japanese still expected her to be at the office at 7 a.m. precisely, every day except Sunday: consequently she was having to rise between 4.30 and 5.30 a.m. Baba usually went with her but if he was ill or too tired, the adopted Indian teenager, Chokra, accompanied her. For the journey she wisely donned man's attire, stuffed her fine long hair under a man's felt hat and carried a man's umbrella. By 2 p.m. each day, if all her duties were done, she could return home. But on rare occasions, if maybe additional Japanese officers were passing through the area and she had to see that someone provided their meals, she and Baba or Chokra would have to remain one night or two in Kanthonezint in her own house.

* * * * *

The Allies were continuing their bombardments of Bassein periodically. It was only about five miles from Thudawgon, so Ma Ma Hta drew out a plan of a *trench* – large enough to accommodate the whole family. She made it circular, and sectioned it off to include a room for sleeping and a 'lounge', kitchen and washroom with toilet. Simple 'beds', 'benches', large 'shelves' and 'kitchen shelves' were dug out of the mud. Those who helped to fit it out positioned it far enough away from the houses to be hopefully free from risk. Later on, some important

Japanese officers happened to notice it and asked whose idea the trench was. They were surprised to find that the Headwoman was responsible and complimented her on its design. She believed that God gave her many good practical ideas during the war years – keeping them all free from harm.

The Watcher knew all about the trench. He also knew that U Chit Htwe rose early every weekday morning after the Headwoman and her companion had started out for Kanthonezint. Day after day he had seen him leave the house carrying a book and going down towards the river (creek). The young man was curious to know why he did it. Maybe he wondered if the old man was sending signals to an enemy.

Ma Ma Hta says: 'My father was very pious you know. Every morning he walked down to the river, to a little beach. Then he just looked up to the sky and prayed for everybody, you know – that sort of thing. He would also sit and read his Bible and meditate for a long time down there at the beach.

'My father cared very much about everyone's soul. He was giving us all Bible teaching lessons – including the children of the others in our community: he taught us at home and also in the Church Hall which was used as a school. He took Services and gave adult Bible Studies there on Sundays.'

As time went by, the young Watcher realised that the Headwoman's father was going down to the beach to pray to God. He was impressed with the holy manner of the elder (as we will learn later on). He probably guessed that he was reading a holy book, because he saw him stop and look up at the sky to pray, time and again.

* * * * *

The Japanese still resented the fact that the Headwoman had chosen to live in Thudawgon. 'They wanted my brother and me under their noses. Once, they had heard that my older brother, who was in the British Indian Army, was going to be dropped by parachute into the Bassein area. This happened to be true, but he didn't actually come. Maybe he was warned not to, by a Burmese spy.

'Their officers set about making me *extremely* busy. It was from the time that I moved that they saw to it that I was kept fully occupied – and had no time for espionage, I suppose! After walking at least five miles to Kanthonezint (Thudawgon to the river – two milles, Bassein to Kanthonezint – three miles) I had to immediately begin work. I had to look after the officers, do odd jobs for them, make sure that the groups of airmen were fed on the days that they arrived, etc.

'One of my duties was to help the Health Officer. About that time where was a growing number of large rats terrorising the area. The Health Officer said that everyone was to catch as many as they could! They either caught or killed them. As an incentive the Japanese offered a reward of two small boxes of matches. They gave me the store of rewards. I was to keep a tally of all those who trapped a rat and issue the rewards. If a person caught more than one, he still only received the same reward. Later, rewards were reduced to one box – and finally, one matchbox for two rats. We knew that the rats could spread the disease of plague – so everyone was pleased. After many difficulties we managed to bring them under control.'

Not long afterwards, the Headwoman was told that one of the *Burmese* men was accusing her of keeping some of the matchboxes for herself! She was angry. She had to answer for herself and clear her name. The accuser was ashamed when he heard her explain that she was very frugal and had always saved all kinds of things since pre-war days. When the Japanese had first come to Kanthonezint they had fairly regularly issued a large box of matchboxes to every household, and oil, and she had saved quite a few boxes, then.

The fact that a Burmese had reported one of her family to the Japanese had saddened Ma Ma Hta. 'I was fed up with my people. We had always stood up for them, and tried to shield them from any of the Japanese excesses – and this was the thanks that we got.' It was a little while before Ma Ma Hta managed to get over the incident. She was deeply affected by it.

10

The Trial of Faith

One morning early, when Ma Ma Hta was about to leave
Thudawgon for work, she was astonished to see the two
Indian *malis* from Kanthonezint hastening towards her
home.

The gardeners had come post haste through the early
hours, to report to the Headwoman that the Japanese Supply Officer, who stayed at the Monastery, had cut short the
legs of her large dining table!

Ma Ma Hta was, of course, furious. She immediately
started out for Kanthonezint with her brother and both of
the men to confront the Supply Officer. She had had words
with him before! The *malis* had told her that they had seen
him sawing off the legs, and that the table was out in the
compound. They said that the Burmese women who had
been designated to help in the preparation of Japanese
pastries and noodles for the army, were using it to roll out
the pastry!

By the time they arrived at Kanthonezint, there were a
few villagers to be seen and male Burmese forced labourers were at work in the sun. They must have noticed Ma
Ma Hta 'half-running, half-walking down the road' – a
cross, determined expression upon her face. Hurrying on
purposefully, she looked neither to the left nor to the right.
She headed straight for the Monastery.

Her brother, who had hardly been able to keep in step with her, left her side to see to his duties elsewhere. (He may have left for Bassein town, to see his friends.) The weary *malis* were dismissed to go to the vegetable field, having done their loyal best for their Headwoman.

The local people must soon have sensed that something unusual was going on. Ma Ma Hta was behaving so differently. Living under the Japanese, they could never be quite sure, at any given time, what would happen next. No doubt many were in daily fear of some catastrophe or other – imagined or otherwise – even though they knew that Ma Ma Hta had often protected them, speaking up for them all. They very likely thought that there was something ominous about the way that she had not even glanced at any of them as she had passed.

The few Japanese soldiers who were present were not seen by her. By now, everyone's eyes were probably upon the lean but strong young woman, striding forward. She reached the Monastery, went through the gateway into the compound and could see the Supply Officer, watching the Burmese women kneading the dough for the sweetmeats etc. – upon her family's finest mahogany dining table! What a sight! She could hardly contain her feelings.

The village onlookers, who loved Ma Ma Hta, had stopped what they were doing – the men who were working as coolies for the Japanese now made a play at labouring – but had their eyes glued on Ma Ma Hta. Her people began shifting slowly towards her, driven by curiosity and yet dread. Something was definitely going on – but what? Trouble was certainly brewing. They were all drawn along as if by a magnet, almost involuntarily edging nearer to Ma Ma Hta, until they came to a stop just outside the Monastery fence, where they could see her clearly.

The soldiers had moved also, but it wasn't to prevent the people from trying to see what would take place. They wanted to know themselves! Although they were now on alert in case of unrest, they had more or less accompanied the spectators! Nothing exciting ever happened in the area, except when the Buddhists celebrated their religious feasts – if allowed to do so by the Japanese.

The Headwoman came to a stop facing the Supply Officer. 'What is the trouble?' he asked her, in a brisk, clear, authoritative voice.

Unfortunately, Ma Ma Hta immediately rounded on him. She began blaming him to his face, for his misdeed. (Extremely overheated after her spirited walk from the river and having made no attempt to control her temper, she had never been so angry in her life. 'I was mad at him!') She attacked him with her tongue: 'I have come to speak to you face to face, about cutting short the legs of *my* dining table!' she accused. 'Who gave you permission to do this?' Pointing at the legs, she didn't wait for an answer: 'You didn't ask me – you just took it out because I am not at home! That is excusable, but why did you cut the legs? Haven't you got any sense – or brain? Instead of cutting the legs to lower the height of it – why didn't you dig holes in the ground, and put the legs in them!' She mimed as she spoke, knowing that he knew very little English.

Ma Ma Hta says in restrospect about the incident: 'I shouldn't have told him off in front of everybody. He was very angry – that was my fault too. He was the only officer there, and I said it with the lower ranks present. I also shamed him in front of the labourers. He became so incensed! He was absolutely livid! When I had finished telling him what I thought, I left him on the spot, not even allowing him to answer for himself. I just went back home. As I went I realised that I had made a mistake.' She was still convinced that he was in the wrong and should have asked her before moving the table: initially, she 'had always offered the table for the use of the Japanese and subsequently told the officers that if they wanted any more furniture for the Monastery they could come and ask' – as there were still some items at home. At that time, the officers had answered 'Yes', as if they had all understood.

* * * * *

Ma Ma Hta was conscious of a sympathetic crowd, as she passed everyone to return home. They had all become a closer community since the Japanese had taken over. She had hardly entered the house when she heard footsteps and saw the Supply Officer marching into her compound. As he had come through the gate, she could see that behind him it looked as though all her people had gathered to support her and were standing in groups along the road in front of her property. They were whispering to one another that *this* time Ma Ma Hta would be 'finished' – others saying that she would be 'killed'. All at once, there was a terrifying pause!

The Supply Officer marched forward to her veranda steps. The young Headwoman appeared in the front doorway. She did not look at all afraid. She looked at the man and said,'Come in.'

He stood before her without speaking.

The atmosphere was tense.

He remained motionless at the base of the steps, glaring up at her with lips pursed and glinting eyes narrowing. She saw that he was still fuming. She was aware that he was in full uniform. She did not notice the sword in its scabbard, at his side.

There was a dreadful hush.

The people were huddling together in terror. The soldiers must have been keenly interested to know the outcome of this unheard-of affair. No woman had ever dared to insult an officer, especially one of the officers of the Japanese Imperial Army. There was bound to be a reprisal. How would he deal with this Headwoman?

There was an electrifying stillness in the vicinity of the compound – though the birds were calling wildly. Ma Ma Hta looked so vulnerable, standing on the veranda, facing the armed officer. 'In my heart I was thinking, "God is with me" – and I experienced no fear at all.'

Looking straight into his eyes, she did not realise that he had removed his sword from its sheath – until she suddenly glimpsed flashing steel, glinting in the brilliant sunlight.

A great, audible gasp went up from the people. All knew that a Japanese officer only withdrew his sword when he was about to use it.

Almost simultaneously Ma Ma Hta's voice rang out across the compound, to the ears of the anxious crowd:

'*You* – sword!' She pointed at the man before her, and then at the sword in his hand.

'*Mainma* (woman) – no sword!' she said, pointing to herself and then to his sword as she shook her head.

'*You* – Japanese officer. You sword – I sword – I fight!' She said miming. 'You gun – I gun – I fight!' she mimed. '*Mainma* – no sword. *You* – coward! *Mainma* not a coward – I fight!' She bared her fist appropriately.

Although his knowledge of English was limited, the Supply Officer comprehended the suggestion that he was a man, armed, and she a defenceless woman, but that she would fight if she had a sword.

He did not strike her!

Instead, he looked up at the roof, then stretched his right arm upwards in a showy gesture, until the sword came into contact with something lodged in the low roof guttering; then he obviously twisted the weapon – presumably to dislodge the obstruction – brought the sword down to his side and returned it to its sheath. He then made a most unexpected move – quickly thrusting out his hand, to shake hers!

Ma Ma Hta says: 'I was still angry. I said, "I never shake hands with a coward!" and shook my head. Most of the people had not understood the words I had used.'

'I – no coward!' he flung back at her, icily.

They wondered why the officer did not *kill* her – and were amazed to see him just turn on his heel and march back to the Monastery 'in a dignified manner'.

'After a few minutes a Japanese soldier came from the Supply Officer with the message: Come and report to the office. I didn't go. I sent the reply: "I will ask *Honjo kikan* about this!"'

It wasn't long afterwards that one of the soldiers arrived at the house, to present the Headwoman with a gift from the Supply Officer! It was sugar, in a billycan. He held it out saying, 'Please take.' Ma Ma Hta said 'No' and shook her head – 'I never take a bribe from anyone. I am a woman.' The young soldier extended his hand dutifully, further towards her. At that, she said curtly, 'Out!' and he backed and hurried away.

After a while, the local people resumed their occupations. The Supply Officer was to be seen approaching the Headwoman's house with something in his hand. He was taking the gift there himself. He went up onto the veranda. Ma Ma Hta emerged, surprised to see him with the gift.

'I am not married. Single *mainma* cannot take a gift from any sort of man,' according to Burmese custom. 'No – I will not take it.' The officer still stood there. As an after-thought she added, 'If you want to give a gift – give it to me at Christmas, or on a birthday' – that was permissible in Burmese society. He could have been familiar with the word 'Christmas'. As he turned to leave she said, 'Thank you for the gesture.' The officer nodded militarily, saluted, and departed.

The Japanese guards had seen strange things that day.

Ma Ma Hta came to realise that her people had been greatly strengthened and encouraged by her bold actions. She remembered two comments in particular: 'Ma Ma Hta – you are very brave!' and 'You are wonderful!' She gave the glory to God.

Surely one is permitted to say that Ma Ma Hta, like so many before her and after her – 'By faith ... escaped the edge of the sword; out of weakness was made strong' (Hebrews 11:33,34).

* * * * *

Ma Ma Hta says that even before the war, if there was no doctor at hand, the local people had relied on her family for simple medical help. Now, whenever an important Japanese officer was in the area, she would approach him to obtain medical aid for ailing Burmese villagers. Two of the doctors who lived in Bassein came, voluntarily, out to Thudawgon to see what the conditions were. (They both happened to be Japanese Methodists.)

The younger one, who was about twenty-five, had visited Ma Ma Hta's parents every day on horseback before they had moved and was happy to see that Daw Ma Ma's health was slowly improving.

The other doctor, who was about thirty-seven years old, learnt from Ma Ma Hta that various patients had been coming to them for help but she couldn't diagnose what was wrong with some of them; and she also said that her stock of medicines was running lower. She asked both of them if they could come to render advice. The older man said that they would endeavour to come on Sundays whenever they could, and asked her to gather the patients together on the veranda of her home in readiness for their visits.

So began a voluntary service of mercy. The younger doctor visited occasionally, but Ma Ma Hta says that the older one gave up a lot of his free time and 'never missed a

Sunday'. Their advice to both Burmese and Karen patients
was invaluable and when they were able they dispensed a
few simple medicines. They were also interested to learn
of the local traditional herbal medicines, mentioned by
Ma Ma Hta, that the people themselves had concocted.
The grateful patients responded, doing the exercises,
massage or whatever was required of them. There were
gradual signs of improvement.

Christmas Day was almost upon them. When the doctors were on a visit, Ma Ma Hta was surprised to hear the
younger one suggest that they go around the villages singing carols on Christmas Eve.

'A couple of days later the doctor came to say that he
could not go carol singing because he had to go somewhere else on 23rd December. He added that he might
come to see me in April or May 1944.'

* * * * *

Ma Ma Hta asked Officer Honjo if she could spend Christmas Day at Thudawgon and was given permission to do
so. She was so glad. She was also very pleased that the
Supply Officer had remembered to bring her the Christmas presents that he had promised her after the sword
episode. She had received the gifts graciously. As she
stood on the steps of her Kanthonezint home, he suddenly
extended his hand to her. She turned to put the presents
down; then, this time smilingly shook hands with him. He
said 'We are friends?' – for a moment looking apprehen-
sive. She answered 'Yes'. Well satisfied, he turned-about,
and marched away.

He had given her a small tin of Ovaltine (with which
one could make delicious chocolate drinks), 'loose coffee',
some unrefined sugar in a billycan: things that were normally unobtainable in Burma at the time. He also presented her with matches. Obviously they were things with
which the Japanese officers were being issued. They had

already raided all the town food stores. In war it was not thought of as robbery, but well-deserved spoil.

Not long after Christmas, Ma Ma Hta held a get-together for the 'over 60s' living in the Thudawgon area. She had been saving food and gifts for the elderly people – who, in Burma, were respected by all. On the day of the party she went to collect both Karen and Burmese Christians and Burmese Buddhists, who didn't have an escort, to the family home. They all arrived to see that there was a Christmas tree outside, with presents hanging upon it, and that the whole longhouse was decorated with Christmas trimmings (all the dividing screens having been removed). 'They were delighted. You should have seen their faces! They had never had anyone give them a special party at their time of life. I was nearly crying.'

The celebration was after the colonial British style. They played party games, which included pass-the-parcel and musical chairs (using floor mats) which they thoroughly enjoyed. Later there was a sing-song and then the family acted, performed a little drama, and sang carols to them. Then they were given what Ma Ma Hta called 'a treat'.

At that stage of the war it was marvellous to have a little extra food. They were given a simple meal. The first course was fresh milk and *jagree* (unrefined brown cane sugar); the main course was yam with shredded coconut; a 'sweet' which consisted of *sugee* (semolina) and more *jagree*; finishing with a mixture of ovaltine and coffee and *jagree* again. It was lovely to taste good old *jagree* again. They were quietened to hear a short Christmas talk from U Chit Htwe who preached Jesus to them. Then they all sang and had prayer to finish the evening.

Before leaving they were overcome with yet another surprise, a precious gift of a small box of matches and two candles from the Christmas tree – 'which to them was like being given gold,' said Ma Ma Hta.

They had had an unusually cheerful few hours. Compared with people in other parts of the country they were quite well off.

* * * * *

In other parts of Burma, many people had no rice, poultry, pigs or cattle and very little to live on. (It wasn't quite so bad in the fertile Bassein area.) There were no imported cotton goods, therefore some people were in rags. There was no salt, matches or cooking oil. The people were suffering from smallpox, skin diseases etc. and malaria was rife. There were no properly functioning hospitals except the Japanese military ones, and no Western medicines. On top of that, Burmese citizens were still being arrested and tortured. A small number of Burmese were spying for the *Kempetai* (information from author Maurice Collis).

In general, by this time, the Burmese population had mixed feelings about this war over Burma, their own beloved land. Ma Ma Hta has revealed something of what the people thought privately:

'It is true to say that the majority wanted the British back in Burma.' (Ma Ma Hta vouches for this.) 'The Japanese had made too many bad mistakes to be accepted and respected. To say the least of it, they were considered to be cruel, barbaric and generally disrespectful of the people and their religious observance – treating many of them virtually as slaves.'

A small minority of the Burmese thought that it would be better to keep the *Japanese* in Burma because they believed they would get independence sooner than under the British. Others thought that the Japanese had disrupted everything, for example, there was far less rice because the Japanese had taken the bullocks which were used to plough the paddy fields.

Ma Ma Hta herself felt the following national resentments at that time: 'There was a general, justified feeling of resentment against the bigger Powers, for causing deaths, carnage and destruction in our own wonderful country of Burma – just because there was a war on between themselves, which really had nothing to do with us – the Burmese.'

Ma Ma Hta (sunglasses) with past deaf students, Rangoon, 1990s

11

Answers to Questions

At Thudawgon the teaching in the school, which was in the Church Hall, had been Christian first and secular second. 'Father gave our younger ones extra tuition at home. At the school for our community he held classes in English and Geography. He did not want the Burmese children to forget their own language, particularly as all children were expected to speak, and also write, in Japanese. One of the Burmese teachers was teaching them to read and write in the Burmese script, to make sure that they knew their own language better than Japanese. One of the other Burmese teachers was very good at Mathematics and taught it successfully.'

There was a big grassy space on one of the hillsides which was used for open-air activities. Ma Ma Hta conceived the idea of having a Sports Day. She included the usual colonial school events that she had been used to as a child, such as various types of races: egg and spoon, 3-legged, skipping, sack and obstacle races. There were also other competitive events. At the end there was a prize giving. All the children who were well enough physically entered into everything and thoroughly enjoyed themselves, their naturally active lives having been restricted under the Japanese in Kanthonezint. The adults too must have benefited as they watched the children laughing so much and saw them unafraid.

* * * * *

As 1944 progressed, Ma Ma Hta continued her long walks to and from work, but they must have been arduous. There were times when she arrived home at 5.30 p.m. and was so exhausted that she just flung herself on her bed, without any supper, and slept through until the morning. She says that she really enjoyed walking in the early mornings, when it was fresh and dewy. Surrounded by the natural beauties of her great God's creative power, she did much praising and praying as she went along. She also thought of Hla Thin, of course, and wondered again where he was and what he was doing. She had no idea that he was at times in one of the busiest and most humid cities in the world – Calcutta – and that at others he was on dangerous missions in their own Burma, in the Intelligence Service of SOE, Force 136, acting for the British.

The Japanese found that the Burmese usually did as they were told, as a people; but, with hindsight, they were never sure who their enemies might be within Burma. They continued to make efforts to befriend the population outwardly but they seemed in general to have been in a quandary as to exactly how to allay Burmese fears and suspicions.

This was one of the reasons why a most unusual thing took place. Ma Ma Hta always believed that God was working in the prevailing atmosphere between the Japanese and the Burmese, in the local situation. There had been much prayer for the Japanese that the family knew.

Two officers had approached Ma Ma Hta and said that they would like to 'have a little meeting' to ask some questions and wanted some advice. They asked if she would take them to her father's place in Thudawgon. On a quiet evening the two officers from the *Honjo kikan* office, one younger, one older – were seen with the Headwoman and her brother approaching U Chit Htwe's house in Thudawgon. Ma Ma Hta says that they were 'nice people'. (She thought they may be Christian.) They were invited in and 'father, my brother and I sat on the floor around a low table with them, in private. The older officer had told me that he wanted to have some advice.'

They would have no time to think what to answer.

'I was surprised and was interested to hear what they were going to tell us. But they didn't seem to have come to tell us anything; they just wanted to ask us questions!'

'Can you advise us as to what to do?' said the older man.

'What? About what?' asked my father in puzzlement.

'The Burmese people... ' he began, looking slightly embarrassed. 'Do they like us?'

Well – what a question!

'Ask *them*,' answered the Headwoman, wisely.

'Do they hate us?' the Japanese asked. U Chit Htwe did not answer.

When they asked about the people in general, she said: 'As for me – we do not hate the Japanese because you all are not our enemy. We love – not hate – people.'

Ma Ma Hta knew that she hated the things done by the *Kempetai* Secret Police. She thought that they didn't know her people; they didn't know anything. As Headwoman, she had a heart for her people and always took care of them, and her family. She knew that the very young Burmese *interpreters* were afraid of the Japanese – and they were also 'too big for their boots'. Consequently some of their 'really learned and respected' people suffered because of the impressions the interpreters gave to the Japanese officers. They sometimes gave the wrong interpretation because they 'never dared say yes or no'. Ma Ma Hta also believed that the Japanese took people for torture simply because they thought that they were the types likely to be pro-British.

'I personally hate nobody,' she said aloud, 'except those who are treating the arrested Burmese so badly.' (She was thinking of the fine Karen ICS officer, their friend, U Ba Tun, who had been tortured even though he hadn't committed any crime.) 'I act in love towards everybody,' she stated. They knew that the family were Christian. The Japanese officers must have known that what she had said was true.

'Do you want to know the truth?' she questioned.

They nodded.

Ma Ma Hta felt that her father wanted her to do the answering, so she went ahead; they knew each other's minds. Her wise father preferred to sit beside her, in prayer about the conversation. He was a prayerful man, always talking with his heavenly Father.

'If you prove yourselves to be better than the British, we will like you all,' began Ma Ma Hta. 'We were brought up under the British over many years. We grew to know and trust them. We wouldn't change suddenly to liking completely different people who had taken charge of Burma.' She presumed that they would recognise the sense in what she had said.

'You want to know how people feel,' she continued, 'We can really only say how *we* see things and I can only tell you about some of the people I happen to know or have met. We do not know how people feel in the rest of Burma. We have no contact with the outside world. Our view is limited.' She was endeavouring to be fair and truthful and set the whole matter in its right context. 'I do not know what other people feel,' she went on, 'but I know why many of them don't like you at all.' They wished to hear the truth and she intended to be frank anyway. (We must not forget the whole situation.

Although it could be very dangerous to speak out, Ma Ma Hta, as a Christian, was never ashamed of telling the whole truth, no matter how unpalatable to the Japanese.) 'We consider you Japanese to be unjust. When taking someone, it has not mattered whether they are guilty or guiltless. Our people have been tortured whether they have spoken the truth or not. Innocent people that we know have suffered unspeakable physical and mental stress. You don't find out the truth as to whether they are free of blame. All get tortured.'

The two officers may not have witnessed the administration of the rough justice at Kanthonezint. They did not defend it, anyway.

'The Japanese got off on the wrong foot to *begin* with,' she continued. 'Those who first came into Burma – into Rangoon, made a big mistake. They walked into the temples with their boots on. The Buddhist Burmese were horrified at the desecration of their places of worship; they always removed their footwear before entering a shrine. Another thing that caused shock was that the soldiers defrocked (deposed) all the Buddhist monks, publicly, which the people thought was a shameful thing to do to their revered religious communities. They also made them wear ordinary clothes instead of saffron robes. Immediately, the people of Burma intensely disliked the Japanese. The fact that they had shown disrespect towards the Buddhist religion went a long way to lowering their opinion of the incoming army. The Japanese increased their bad behaviour by making all the monks into coolies, to fetch and carry for them. The Buddhists could not forgive this.' (This was in spite of *Japan* being a Buddhist country at that time.)

The two officers had not seen such goings on in the Bassein district. They were 'nice men' and may not have approved of such things. Not all Japanese in Burma were the same. They did not comment on what Ma Ma Hta had told them.

'We do not like the fact that most of our Burmese men, and Indians and Chinese, have been forced to serve you. They are not respected. They have to be coolies, and give the Japanese everything they demand, and obey whatever they are commanded to do. We are supposed to have an independent country but both men and women are usually treated like slaves. How can we like you for such treatment?' It was a rhetorical question.

'Our people were, and still are, stunned. We are still getting over the loss of our previous *Asoya* (Burmese government under the British). The Japanese officers that we have met *here* are really gents, compared with some of the others.'

The officers must have been gratified to hear that!

Ma Ma Hta's father assented to her remark.

'Another thing – the Japanese are mean when it comes to paying for people's labour. Also, our people thought that your soldiers were very rude and disrespectful. We Burmese are taught that the head is the most respected and sacred part of the body. None of us like the Japanese habit of face-slapping and boxing people's ears in public. They feel very angry.' She had thought that they would do the same to her father, if he became Headman.

'We want to know how we can change our ways. What can we do to find favour with the Burmese people – so that we can understand each other more?' asked the older officer courteously.

'I think it is too late now. The damage is done. When you want to know about the Burmese people's reactions to you, we really cannot answer for them. As for us – the Christians here, we are talking to you from our hearts. As for the other people – they must answer for themselves.'

U Chit Htwe also agreed with what his daughter had just said. The session was almost at an end.

(Ma Ma Hta told me: 'When the Japanese officers at the *Kempetai* office used to ask me why I was doing so many things for them – all the voluntary help – it was a puzzle to them. I told them straight – "We are Christians." They then came to know that I am very honest and that I am doing good to them in good faith, in sincerity and with good-will.')

Every time, when the two officers who came to Thudawgon asked straightforward questions, Ma Ma Hta asked them: 'Do you trust us? Do you accept what we are going to say when it comes to suggesting things to do? Will you take it that we are telling you what we know, and what we know in our hearts?'

The two officers had replied, 'Oh yes – that is why we have come here.'

'You are honest and you are doing good to us,' added the second man.

'The Japanese soldiers are against the Burmese and Christian laws – so we cannot condone what they do,' stated Ma Ma Hta frankly.

The officers stood up to leave. They had the information they needed, presumably. The expressions on their faces were noticeably more serious than when they had first arrived. They were at the point of departure, when the first officer asked suddenly, 'What about the Christian men at the YMCA? Are they willing to be used, to help us?'

'I cannot tell you exactly. I don't know,' said the Headwoman, warily. Then she issued a friendly warning: 'If you want us to change our minds about your general behaviour in this country, you will have to prove that you are better than the British. You cannot educate us. We Burmese are quite well educated. Prove to us that you are better now. Anyway, it's a bit late – I think.'

* * * * *

Ma Ma Hta had omitted mentioning to the two question-
ers the fact that the Burmese local people had been really
shocked to see Japanese airmen coming along the road to
her own well – to wash – in nothing but a G-string. In other
parts of Burma the Japanese men and women thought
nothing of being naked as they went to bathe in the river
or elsewhere.

Another thing was the fact that the Burmese considered
that the Japanese were barbaric and had no manners: for
example, when they slurped their food – and had a habit
of mixing tea with cane sugar into their rice!

She could have reminded both of the officers of the
times when their troops went wild and stole the belongings of the Burmese villagers.

They had also taken good teak furniture out of their
school and used it to make fires when cooking. Once, she
had stopped one of the young soldiers from completely
smashing up the monastery bookcase for firewood. By her
attitude, she had tried to show him that he should not des-
ecrate something that had been set aside for religious
purposes.

(The author, Leslie Glass, wrote that the military used
the Christians' large Cathedral in Rangoon as a brewery.)

There were many other misdeeds committed by the Japanese that appalled and disgusted the people of Burma.

* * * * *

One day Ma Ma Hta had to present herself at the *Honjo
kikan* office. She received a totally unexpected order
issued by one of the officers. He wanted her to 'change the
face of the ground' – in other words help the Japanese with
a particular camouflage. There was an imposing bungalow, situated in the middle of the customary Burmese
cultivated land, called gardens.

The Japanese Officer, *Honjo*, trusted her so he told Ma
Ma Hta that a 'very important person' – a General, whom

he called a 'Prince' – was to rest in the house that very night. It was therefore imperative to plant 100 banana trees in the garden surrounding it – to make it appear to be a plantation. The work had to be accomplished by 10 p.m. that evening; the time was then about 10 a.m. Ma Ma Hta was not worried about that but she found herself facing a dilemma. She was expected positively to assist the Japanese against the British (and her fiancé was loyal to the British). If she did not carry out the order the lives of her family members would be in danger.

As she sent for her assistant, Maung Ohn Shwe, and the two Indian gardeners that the Japanese had provided her with to grow vegetables for the eight airmen, she was thinking: 'Anyway the Japanese are too late! The British in their reconnaissance planes must have taken several photographs of the surrounding district already.' The camouflage would not be much of a problem. She was sure that the British would naturally put two and two together. Both sides in the conflict camouflaged military sites of course.

Ma Ma Hta comments on this task: 'Appointed as Headwoman – it was my responsibility to do something. I was in their hands in one sense. Whatever they asked I had to do much of the time, or even my neighbours would probably have had to suffer otherwise.' She had heard of many reprisals meted out by the Imperial Japanese Army.

'When I came back to Kanthonezint from Bassein, I called for my assistant, Ohn Shwe, and told him what was to be done. I ordered him to collect as many youngish big and small banana plants as he could. He would have to borrow them from the villagers who all grew bananas in their garden plots. He must pick the most suitable ones and dig them up. But first of all, he was to take several from my own garden; then afterwards make the number up to one hundred from generous local people.'

Ohn Shwe did as he was told, making many trips to the field as he piled the banana trees onto Ma Ma Hta's and his own bullock carts and then drove them there; then he carried each one to the holes that were being dug in the field for their reception.

The two Indian *malis* were with Ma Ma Hta in the green gardens. At first they watched the Headwoman beginning to stride out to mark out the ground with 2 ft squares (measured with her forearm). Soon they were digging the holes to a depth of 2 ft. 'I was thankful to God that the soil was moist enough to make it easier for the men to do the job more quickly.' After digging, they planted each tree then shovelled back the loose earth firmly. Ma Ma Hta was carefully choosing the order and size of each plant so that the garden was to look as natural a banana plantation as possible. She also carried out some of the planting. Towards the front of the bungalow she had the tallest trees mixed with a few smaller ones. At the back, she had arranged smaller and very young ones plus a good number of the more established fruit trees. So the bungalow was suitably secluded.

Ohn Shwe was used to hard labour; he was a farmer who had a paddy field. For almost eight hours the two Indian *malis* sweated, under pressure in the heat of the day, to finish all the digging and planting. Their everyday work was gardening but they had never had to carry it out so strenuously.

Without the Headwoman's swift planning, commonsense, determination and encouragement, the task could not have been accomplished so effectively.

Ma Ma Hta went along to the *Kempetai* office to report that all had been completed – earlier than their task master had anticipated! The officer must have breathed a sigh of relief because the very important General was about to arrive at any moment. The bungalow was to be put at his disposal directly.

The Kanthonezint villagers, who had promptly let Ohn Shwe make use of their precious trees – not really expecting them ever to be returned – were later commended very warmly by Ma Ma Hta for their unselfish community effort. They all rejoiced and celebrated together as they beheld the splendid result – a new banana plantation worthy of the name!

* * * * *

The Headwoman received a message that the Japanese wanted her to be at the *Honjo kikan* office in Kanthonezint at 11 a.m. Now what could be the reason for that? One never knew with the Japanese.

Ma Ma Hta arrived on time at the office, which was in a bungalow. It was one of the finest bungalows, commandeered by the Japanese for use as accommodation plus office for *Honjo* and three other officers.

As she was ushered into the lounge, Ma Ma Hta was surprised to see the Prince there. He was sitting in a relaxed position with Honjo and three or four of his officers who were around the room, who were also seated. He was obviously pleased to see her. As she stood in the middle of the room, he offered her a chair and began to talk to her in a friendly way. 'I wanted to see you to thank you very much for your help,' he began, after their short chat – 'and the officers are very pleased with you, as well.'

'It's been all my pleasure,' she said graciously.

'When I was told that the Headwoman had made the plantation I was amazed,' the Prince exclaimed. 'I never thought a woman could have accomplished such a project – producing an entire banana plantation – and in such a short space of time! Ma Ma Hta, it is wonderful! – you, as a woman, can manage all these things.' There were murmurs of praise from the men present. (According to Ma Ma Hta, all the military staff at that bungalow had also been amazed at the transformation achieved by herself and her assistants.)

'You are very quick; and very clever – putting tall trees around the house,' the Prince enthused. 'You are very efficient – marvellous! I am very, very pleased – very pleased!' (His enthusiasm could have inferred that it had been a means of possibly even saving his life.)

All the officers were beaming at her.

Ma Ma Hta continued to arise and bow, at every compliment paid.

'We are extremely thankful. Just because we are grateful we wished to thank you personally.'

'I thank you *very* much,' she replied, bowing low with respect, once again. The Prince smiled and she smiled radiantly in return. The officers were silent as she backed slowly towards the door and was allowed out into the sunshine.

(Ma Ma Hta says about this whole incident: 'That was all God's plan. Psalm 23 was always in my mind, whatever I've done, whatever I do – everything is within *his* plan.)'

12

The General's Speech and Banquet

In Thudawgon – days later – Ma Ma Hta told her father that Honjo had confided that there was to be a meeting of all the Headmen in the southwest Bassein area, presided over by a visiting General – who was a Prince! Strange to say it was to be held right there, in Thudawgon of all places! She wondered whatever had made them choose to have it in such an inaccessible spot.

When a Japanese officer came to the house to invite her to the meeting and a banquet afterwards, she said, 'If you want me to come, I can only do so if you also invite my brother or my father.' Every Headman had to give his name. Ma Ma Hta included her brother.

Upon the designated day, a number of extra soldiers arrived in the district in advance to prepare for the gathering. Naturally, the people of the Burmese-Karen village, as well as those of the adjoining Burmese settlement, were all abuzz at the news. What were the Japanese up to this time? They had heard all kinds of evil things concerning them.

The Japanese were taking over the larger Karen Baptist Chapel for the occasion – not the one that the family had helped to construct. The other one was built of solid teak, supported on long struts (poles). The roof was of corrugated iron which could become searingly hot at times. In the fine structure, there would be space for at least 200 people, and a few more up on the dais where there were chairs and a table for the dignitaries.

By mid-morning, there was a moving stream of Headmen passing through Thudawgon – most of them noticeably older than Ma Ma Hta. They had all intended to be punctual for the meeting, yet some of them may have had to 'go by the height of the sun' for time, because of the random confiscation of wristwatches by the Japanese in Burma.

The Headmen who had arrived earlier in the day had already gone to relax and refresh themselves at the shaded 'area of rest' – provided in every village – where there would be a large earthenware vessel of water set upon a high stool, and shielded from the sun by a small thatched roof. This provision of places of rest for strangers, with drinkable water, was a Buddhist custom.

It was the hottest season – in the months of March and April.

The meeting was to commence at noon. The Headmen were approaching the chapel in a leisurely fashion, and being ushered up the steps and into the Christian place of worship, where they seated themselves. Many may have been curious to see the inside of the building – as they were Buddhists. They all were dressed similarly, with sober-hued, finely-checked cotton *longyis* (ankle-length skirt made of a length of material sewn down one side), and above this a very white cotton shirt, over which was an *eingyi*, a black cotton mandarin-collared jacket. Their feet were shod with leather sandals. They had no headgear, having chosen not to wear their best clothes at any time during the Japanese occupation of their country.

When the spacious chapel was almost full, the only female 'Headman' appeared, followed by her sister – who wanted to hear what the General was going to say – and

Ma Ma Hta's brother, who was her escort. It would have been most unseemly for a Burmese woman to have entered unchaperoned into such a situation. The men probably wondered why women were allowed to be present; some may have heard that she was appointed by the Japanese. Having chosen to make her way to the back row, the young Headwoman settled herself behind them all, against the wooden wall. She could see that the windows were open, on both sides of the chapel, but could feel no movement of air. Then she noticed that quite a few of the Headmen were sitting on top of the benches, on their haunches, and felt ashamed that her countrymen were behaving so ignorantly when a very important person was about to enter the room.

Ma Ma Hta was also simply dressed – but now she was wearing women's clothes. She had on a plain white, fine muslin *eingyi*, buttoned with five tiny buttons. Her *longyi* was of colourful flowered satin. Round her waist was a two-inch-wide black sash. Normally, she would also have worn a delicate, shimmering shawl, thrown across her shoulders at the front. Black velvet sandals with platform soles (*pain dan* slippers for formal occasions) were on her dainty feet. Her carefully oiled black hair was brushed into a neat bun at the nape of her neck; she did not wish to adorn it with flowers while the Japanese were in command. Her sister was dressed in similar fashion, but in the tresses of her hair was a single, perfumed jasmine blossom. It was the daily habit of most Burmese ladies to wear fresh-picked flowers. All but the poverty-stricken wore jewellery made with real gems in everyday life, but of course these were now hidden away.

* * * * *

At 12 noon precisely, the honoured guest who was to speak to the Assembly arrived with a procession of Burmese local civilian officials, Dr San C. Paw, and Japanese military officers. The Headmen, rising to their feet, observed the striking figure in the full dress uniform of a General, as he solemnly stepped up onto the wide dais and was offered the central position, remaining standing to attention as the retinue moved each to their appointed places. A senior Japanese officer spoke up, introducing the General as 'Prince ...'. (In Japanese the word 'prince' can have a wider use.) Was he really a royal Prince? If so, the Headmen were probably more inclined to listen to him.

The Prince, facing his mature audience, seemed to notice every individual, including of course the Headwoman of Kanthonezint. All had to bow before him. He then sat down, which was the signal for the Headmen to do the same.

In a moment or two, the Prince rose, and in an unhurried, pleasant, resounding voice began his speech with a few introductory remarks, thanking everyone for coming. The Headmen – hearing the words through a Burmese interpreter – were hardy, seasoned, and suspicious of his highly courteous approach. Ma Ma Hta was hoping that the interpreter (who happened to be her future brother-in-law!) would translate exactly, giving the true meaning of his message. She was thinking clearly and weighing up the General's whole attitude. Maybe he sensed something of his listeners' mistrust, as he said, 'I came here for the express purpose of speaking only to you – the Headmen of this area – not to anyone else.'

He went on: 'We have come to this country – not to take over – not to govern – but just because your house is on fire. We are the neighbours who have only come to help you out. You are all our neighbours. If a neighbour's property is on fire – we are constrained to put it out. We are all from the East, so we have an affinity – we belong to one another. We have come to *help* you. We are the friends, we are the neighbours.'

(Ma Ma Hta now says, translating her thoughts, during his speech, into the modern idiom – 'This is something like a brainwash!' At the time she was also remembering the fine Christian Karen retired Civil officer who was their nearest neighbour at Kanthonezint, being tortured by the Japanese when he was innocent of any charge.)

'We have not come to give you any trouble,' the Prince continued. 'At the present time you might feel that we are very hard – but we are not really like that: this is *war*. We people are not cruel and we wish to make friends with you, like neighbours.'

(The elders and Ma Ma Hta knew that the Japanese had been brutal and were disciplining their people to a savage degree. Even in years past, when the Burmese had come across the odd Japanese doctor, accountant, photographer – Mr Kongo in Bassein – who had appeared harmless enough – they had found them to be spies.)

'Don't take it seriously, when people say that we are here to take your soil,' the Prince continued. 'Don't think that we are only saying that we are helping in order to fool you – so that in days to come, we keep your land. We are here to give you a hand and to protect you.'

The General paused for a moment, then said, 'You say, "Don't come here to educate *us*" – but in reply to that we answer that we are helping you out. Yet you people don't respond at all well to us. You all take it amiss. You are just like that. You are like children. We offer you a present or something – you like that.' The Prince sought to make it clear to them how they were reacting – as he saw it – to the Japanese, making it more difficult for the army to get on with its business. He now drove the point home: 'But sometimes you are like dogs – who will only do what is required if someone claps his hands – you then respond like a dog does and will go and bite someone automatically. You listen to your Master (meaning the British),

whether he's good or not. You are biting the Japanese for
the British. Or you're like children, expecting gifts before
you give anything. When you have sweets, then you will
do what we ask.'

It was taking some time to get these rather laboured
points over, because all had to be spoken through an
interpreter.

Ma Ma Hta was becoming more and more incensed – as
no doubt were the Burmese elders – especially when they
were being compared to such things as dogs. The
Headwoman did not make any effort to hide her feelings.
It was quite obvious to the speaker that she was really
angry. He probably would not have been able to read the
expressions on the faces of the rest of the company before
him quite so easily. He ended his talk with more conciliatory words, then made a final appeal to the Burmese,
directly: 'We want you to *help* us.' Without exactly
demeaning himself by pleading with them, he issued a
more friendly appeal – ending his speech by saying,'We
need your co-operation.'

There was silence.

The meeting was at an end. The Prince sat down, and
spoke a word or two to those sitting beside him. He then
rose to leave the dais, accompanied by his retinue as the
Headmen stood in silent respect until the VIPs went out
into the stifling humidity of mid-afternoon.

One of the officers dismissed the assembly, who then
took their time to vacate the chapel. They were quiet.
These knowing men were wise enough not to give any
hint to the Japanese as to what they thought of the ideas
put to them by the illustrious General.

Ma Ma Hta and the other two soon left the chapel.
Her brother had always suffered physically in the
extreme heat. The temperature was somewhere near
100 degrees. Through sitting for so long under the

baking corrugated iron roof, he was faint and uncomfortable. Nevertheless, he remained dutifully with his sisters. They were watching the Headmen dispersing, and noticing that the preparation for the banquet was nearing completion. Several somewhat gaunt and malnourished young soldiers were hastily putting the finishing touches to the very long, white-tableclothed trestle tables that they had erected under the lush tropical trees. They were meticulously arranging the last place-settings for the guests.

The Prince and the other honoured visitors were deep in conversation as they strolled towards the banqueting area.

One of the local Japanese officers approached Ma Ma Hta to lead her to her appointed place at the main table, as her brother left the scene with his sister. The guests were moving to stand behind their chairs at the tables. The guiding officer led the Headwoman to the longer, middle table where she was to stand right opposite the Prince!

When all were positioned, the General made a move to sit down. As he did so, succeeded by the whole company – he looked across at Ma Ma Hta and smiled. She smiled, too.

The young woman realised that she was the only *Headman* present, and what's more, the only woman! She consciously trusted in God her Saviour and therefore would not worry. After a little while, her brother returned and was shown to his place, further down the table on her left-hand side. She was glad that he was back.

The Prince was talking to his Chiefs of Staff and those who had been on the dais at the chapel, as he was being served with delicious Japanese delicacies. Then he turned to the Headwoman – addressing her as Ma Ma Hta! She was reticent, but courteous, with the typical Burmese reaction shown by a younger person towards an older. She couldn't forget what he had said a short while ago about the Burmese people. He spoke again, gradually adopting a more friendly tone and changed to speaking in English, dispensing with the interpreter. (He had had an American education and also probably knew that Ma Ma Hta's father was the Headmaster who had not been able to take up the duties of a Headman.) She was used to being called Ma Ma Hta – everyone seemed happy with it – but it did seem strange, coming from a Prince! He told her that he was pleased with her good service to the Japanese. (She considered that, as a Christian, she of course helped the Japanese – as she would help anyone.) He said that he had heard of her hard work, in carrying out her duties as Headwoman.

As the dinner progressed, diners relaxed and tongues became looser, though there were only fresh fruit juices upon the table. There was more chatter and laughter. The feast was like an oasis in the desert of war, at a time of extreme tension for them all.

Now the Prince, and others who knew English or Burmese, were talking more freely to the young Headwoman – especially the Prince who was speaking 'easily – as to a friend' (she says).

'Ma Ma Hta, how old are you?' he asked.

'Thirty-one,' she replied.

'Are you single?' he wanted to know. 'Why aren't you married yet?' This was a perfectly normal question to ask in the East, where so many married at an early age.

All at once, there was a noticeable hush, as the rest of the company at the table wished to hear the answer.

'I am engaged. My fiancé is with the British Army.'

There was a sudden stillness in the men.

'What is he – a Captain?' continued the Prince.

'When he left, he was a Lieutenant,' she told him. (Maybe the General knew more about her fiancé's present

rank than she did!) She added, 'What's the use of marrying when there's a war on!'

'We, too, have very good Captains!' he said humor-
ously. 'What about *our* men of rank?! There are so many
fine Captains in my forces!' He was laughing – and the
men laughed with him. 'Do you want one? If you want, I
can supply you with one!' There was more hilarity.

'No, thank you,' said the Burmese Headwoman, defen-
sively. 'I would *never* marry a person outside of my own
people!'

'Why didn't you marry earlier?' countered the General.

'I have been waiting – for my man,' she explained. She
was not to be trifled with by the 'conquering foe', no matter how friendly. (Those present must have admired the
young woman for her unswerving audacity, in such company. Ma Ma Hta's comment about her attitude at that
time, is: 'I was praying that I might have courage to say the
truth. At the feast – I said everything I wanted to say.')

The conversation became general again, but the Prince
apparently intended to learn more, for military reasons.

'Why didn't you go to live in *Bassein*, instead of coming
to live here?' Still friendly, he happened to lower his voice.
(Ma Ma Hta says that the Burmese officers next to her
were, maybe, wondering what the General was saying to
her.) The Commander of the army knew that one of her
brothers was also in the British forces, in India. ('All the
Japanese knew about our family.') He had been told of the
suspicions of the local Japanese officers, with regard to
spying. If so, why had the Headwoman given so much
help to the Japanese? Was it just a ploy – so that the family
would not be suspected? No one knew what the General
was thinking. He went on to ask her about her family, and
why she moved to Thudawgon.

'Because my mother was not well – and Bassein was
being bombed. I would have been a fool to have stayed

there. Besides, it's more healthy here for my family. This is a lovely hilly place, with fresh air blowing across the fields much of the time, and with fresh water in the streams. When we had to dig a well, the water soon came out. There are also doctors here, and teachers. We all enjoy it here.'

The Prince agreed that it was more healthy there. He said, 'Why did your community choose a *Karen* village?'

'If we go and live amongst the Burmese people who are of *Burman* origin, some of them will tell you Japanese that we are too British. But here, with the Karens we are all Christian – Burmese and Christian – and so we do not have misunderstandings with them like that. We know that we are the same, even though they are from a Karen background and our family are from the Mons. So we chose this place.'

The General then changed the subject, and did so by letting her know that during his speech at the meeting in the afternoon, he had seen her anger.

'I saw your eyes flashing!' he said.

She had the courage to tell him why she had been furious.

'Yes, I am very angry. I didn't like what you were saying when you compared us with dogs.' She maintained that the Burmese were not like children – in a derogatory sense – and certainly nothing like dogs. His comment was, 'That is very good.' He then smiled, saying 'Yes. I saw you. Yes! Yes! Yes!' – as if he was enjoying the thought of it. He was smiling broadly. She also smiled, although she still had the words of the speech ringing in her ears and felt the insult of it to her people.

During the feast, the Prince called attention to her good work, saying, 'Ma Ma Hta – big sister – you are very quick and very clever. You are wonderful!' (probably alluding to the camouflage), and complimenting her upon all her achievements at Kanthonezint.

The sun was going down. As the daylight decreased, darkness was falling fairly rapidly – as it does in the tropics. Light was being replaced by the ever-increasing sub-light of the moon. Moonlight's silently pervading presence crept slowly over the scene, making its way past and through the lush, scented foliage surrounding the banqueting area, and settling, without a 'by-your-leave', onto every visible stick and stone on the dampening earth.

The organised Japanese switched on the electric lights which they had strung on wires attached to the encircling trees.

Ma Ma Hta had been speaking again, of some of the misunderstandings between ethnic groups. She ended by saying: 'It is better to go and live where everyone worships the same God – under the circumstances.'

This remark seemed to please those who were sitting near the Prince, especially her mention of worshipping God.

The General then said: 'Let us vacate this place and go and listen to the band.'

Ma Ma Hta says: 'So we all got up and went – as we had been asked to do. There were the three Burmese Officers (including the Health Officer), Dr San C. Paw's son, me and my brother – then all the Japanese present. I sat next to the Prince, facing the band, and my brother was sitting near two Japanese officers.' The band began to play.

During the banquet Ma Ma Hta had been told by her future brother-in-law, the interpreter, that the Prince had said quietly in Japanese, to one of his Chiefs of Staff, 'If they had all been like her – with that indomitable spirit – we would not have been able to take Burma!'

* * * * *

When the Japanese Military Band concert was about to come to an end, someone approached the Head-woman bearing the news that her brother was lying

unconscious at home. She had not realised that he had
even left her on her own. Immediately she wanted a
doctor to see him. The man suggested that he should go
and get a Karen doctor from the nearby Karen village.
But she wisely asked for a Japanese medical officer,
thinking that in such company it was 'not nice' to send
for a Karen: she also sought to quell the idea that her
brother might be a spy feigning illness in order to over-
hear inadvertent conversation or something.

Ma Ma Hta told the Prince what had happened, and
excusing herself she took her leave of him, backing courteously away. The interpreter came to take her to the Medical Corps doctors. Two of them accompanied her to the
house. It was a bright moonlit night. They soon came to
the village. Ma Ma Hta could make out several shadowy
military figures posted here and there. The house itself
was surrounded with guards. She thought that they
seemed prepared for some sort of trouble, but maybe there
were extra troops in the vicinity because of the Prince and
the banquet. The group were stopped outside the house
and questioned as if they were spies.

As they entered it, one of the doctors who knew Ma Ma
Hta's mother who was at the door, noticed how careworn
she looked. As he passed her, he whispered in English, 'Do
not worry. He will be all right.'

'Where is the patient?' asked the other. Ma Ma Hta
showed them through to the veranda. As her brother had
been grossly overheated during the speech, the family had
moved him to where there were breezes. He lay almost
motionless and appeared deathly pale.

'We wish to examine him in private. Leave us,' said one
of them. So she left them and went to talk to her parents.
The rest of the family were in their bedrooms.

Daw Ma Ma had been through terrible mother's fears
and had not really expected her daughter to return from

the banquet that night. She definitely did not trust the Japanese. She was relieved to hear all that had taken place. She probably felt rather proud of Hta Hta's behaviour and wise answers to the Prince. But now Baba was so ill. Why hadn't her daughter brought a Karen doctor? She would be glad when this horrible war was over.

Ma Ma Hta went back to find out whether the doctors had made a diagnosis. They said that he would be all right, but that they couldn't do any more for him as they had no syringe to give him an injection. They were surprised when the Headwoman answered brightly, 'I have everything,' and turned to bring what was required, after disinfecting the object. They sat waiting for the patient to come` round. He had become cold and seemed 'quite bad' so they kept calling his name and saying 'Can you hear?' It was more than an hour before the young man recovered; then they injected him.

Ma Ma Hta's mother knew that the doctors liked fresh cows' milk. She warmed some for them as the night was chill. They were grateful and comforted her saying, 'Don't be anxious. Don't worry.' They stayed on longer until they reckoned that he was over the worst.

'We said thank you very much when they left. It was well after midnight.' As they walked down the slope from the house they told the soldiers that it was a 'genuine case' – as they were suspicious of the whole family. The doctors took the soldiers with them.

Daw Ma Ma said to her husband, 'Yes, God is with her.' Ma Ma Hta said, 'Well, if he wasn't, they could do something to harm us.'

Not long after the doctors had gone, a messenger came to tell the Headwoman that she was to be at the *Kempetai* headquarters in Bassein at Mr Congo's house at 7 a.m. the next day! She had no idea why. She didn't like to worry her

mother further. The Japanese were usually unpredictable.
'What for?' she asked him.
   'For questioning.'
   'OK,' Ma Ma Hta said blithely.

13

Interrogation

Before Ma Ma Hta was to leave for Bassein, her parents went with her to the door to see her off. Her mother was naturally upset. Being under the Japanese was a stressful time – anything could happen.

Ma Ma Hta sought to put her mind at rest: 'Mummy, what of it! I'm always speaking the truth to them – and what has ever happened to me?'

'Why worry about her?' her father said. 'We're always praying every day.'

'Nothing tells me not to go,' stressed his daughter.

But Daw Ma Ma was not satisfied with that; she could not resist saying, 'Hta Hta, be careful what you say. You know your mouth is too wide. Don't make him angry!'

'She's all right,' interrupted her husband. 'Don't fret. God is with her.' As she turned to go, he stepped forward towards Hta Hta and said quietly, in faith, 'I'm not worried about you. God is with you,' and with those words in her mind she and her young companion – one of the Karens' sons – walked away to the trodden jungle path leading straight to the Bassein river.

Ma Ma Hta heard afterwards that a Christian aunt who was within the house had also said to her mother, 'Don't be afraid – she will come back.' Also, as they waited, Dr San C. Paw's son, Ovi, happened to pass by.

When he heard about the interrogation he immediately said, 'Don't worry Auntie, Ma Ma Hta will be all right; I know her very well. They will never get the better of *her*!' – as he continued on his way, laughing. She herself had spent much time in prayer, pleading help from her heavenly Father about the coming session at Mr Kongo's house in Bassein.

Being well aware of her natural self-confidence, Ma Ma Hta was all the more careful to cast herself entirely upon the Lord. Without him – she could 'do nothing' (John 15:5), but with God all things (were) possible within his will (Matthew 19:26).

* * * * *

Ma Ma Hta arrived at 7 o'clock. She was shown into Mr Kongo's lounge. She was confronted by a stocky Japanese officer, whom she had seen once before, in the Chapel, on the day the Prince gave his speech. He was a member of the *Kempetai* (Secret Police). She thought he looked 'like a bulldog!'

'What is this all about?' she asked Mr Kongo, the photographer, who was to be the interpreter!

'He wants to ask you some questions,' he replied, brusquely. But the interrogator didn't start immediately.

'It has gone seven already,' she said to Mr Kongo, in a business-like way. 'Shall we begin?'

The interrogator asked Mr Kongo what she was saying. Her words were repeated. If he was taken aback, he did not show it.

Then she continued, (speaking to the interpreter) 'Before we do, there's one thing I want him to know. I intend to answer everything rightly – that is, if I know whatever it is. I'll give him the right answer – whether he believes me or not. I will tell only the truth. But if I answer his questions, is he going to believe what I say? If not, then there will be no point in asking anything. It would be better not to ask any questions at all. On the other hand ...' The words were conveyed to 'the bulldog'.

She suddenly saw that he was 'really very furious!' (Two girls in the back room were listening behind the door. They were terrified for Ma Ma Hta.)

The Japanese Interrogation Officer was almost beside himself with rage. He glared at the slight, calm, upright figure of the Burmese woman before him – then looked at the interpreter and said between clenched teeth: 'I have been all over Burma – north, south, east and west – but no-one has ever *dared* to speak to me like this one!' The translator beside him remained silent.

The officer calmed himself. He then proceeded to question the Headwoman. He knew details of her family, but wanted to know where each one was, at that very time.

Ma Ma Hta mentioned that the eldest was Superintendent at the YMCA in Rangoon, and added that he was also the Commissioner for Scouts throughout Burma. She said that her youngest brother was a jailor in Moulmein and that since university days, he was one who had followed Aung San – 'as many students did'. She told him that an older brother and her fiancé were in the Indian Army, and British Army, in India. Then she told him who was living in her home in Thudawgon.

'Why did you evacuate to the other side of the river and go to live among the Karens?' he asked.

'Why not?' she replied. 'We are Christians. Over there, we can teach our children religion as well as the usual educational subjects.'

Her questioner appreciated that point. 'That is very good,' he said.

Then he asked if the Burmese people hated the Japanese. 'I cannot speak for them all, but I will tell you that they do not like you torturing innocent people,' came the reply.

'Do you prefer the British or the Japanese?'

'We were under the British for many years – brought up and educated with them. I like them because we understand each other. If I do not know you, how can I say I like you? We were living with the British for many years.'

Japanese Intelligence had made him aware that the Headwoman's military brother had been expected to drop down by parachute into the immediate area.

'Have you seen any British parachutists here?'

Ma Ma Hta's family had been appraised of the prospective drop – by a Burmese man from Bassein. She was surprised that 'the Bulldog' knew of it.

'Do you think you have seen a signal? Did you go with a torch, to signal to their aircraft?'

'We dare not go out after the curfew at 6 p.m. How can we see or do anything? I stay inside. I keep the curfew. I didn't hear anything either.' She paused. 'Now please trust me – believe me. If my brother does come as a parachutist, you don't have to worry – I will surrender him to you personally. I won't allow anyone else to do it.'

The man was amazed!

'That's just what I was about to ask! She is telling us everything!' he said to Kongo, in astonishment.

(Ma Ma Hta says, 'I was right to the point. They wondered why I would say a thing like that! I thought that if he came, and we concealed him from them – they would kill us all! There might be a possibility, a little bit of a chance that, if I told the truth – they might let him go free.')

'The Bulldog' suddenly altered his tone.

'Why are you so popular among our Japanese officers?' he asked.

'What? *Am* I so popular with the Japanese officers? In what way do you mean – in good ways or bad?' she replied, pointedly.

'Oh – in good ways. Whatever they ask you, you always tell them, and you are always helping them. Whatever they want, you give them – like food for the airmen etc.'

'Well, I ordered someone to prepare it all for me, and all I had to do was to give it.'

'How do you manage to live? None of you work.' She suspected that he was trying to find out whether she was being paid to spy for the British.

When she replied that she bartered articles, such as *longyis*, he was amused. (She didn't think he ought to know that she had a personal, small store of precious gems. Almost every Burmese woman wore genuine jewels. Burma was a prosperous country in those days.) 'I barter, say, one *longyi* for a tin of oil. With mosquito netting we make blouses to exchange for necessities. We are not reduced to rags. God is good. He supplies enough rice. The Japanese let us have cooking oil. We get salt from the sea water.'

Both the interrogator and Mr Kongo had been laughing over the bartering.

'Can I go now?' asked the Headwoman.

Without replying, the officer moved to one side of the room. He picked up a decorative box of Pond's Dusting Powder (used by the ladies at the time), together with a single packet containing several small boxes of matches, and a beautifully coloured satin *longyi*.

'Please take them,' he said, offering her them.

'I cannot accept,' she answered shortly.

Immediately his anger flared up again – she was insulting him!

'Why?' he retorted, in disbelief.

'Because of what the Prince said yesterday in his speech. He said that we Burmese are like children – only doing things for reward. His words are still ringing in my ears. He said that we were like dogs – only doing tricks for our master if we were given a biscuit. How *can* I accept? If I do, I am like a dog!'

'No, no, no – not because of that. We wish to present these gifts to you out of respect.'

'Oh well, in that case I accept,' she said graciously, giving him one of her dazzling smiles. He was very pleased and smiled in return.

However, he laid the presents down on the table for a while – and spoke once again.

'Ma Ma Hta, we want you to be a spy – for us. We will give you 12,000 *chetts* for it.'

She was extremely surprised. 'So *that* was it,' she thought.

'I'm not interested in being a spy. You know, I am a sort of missionary and I teach love. I am just a teacher of the deaf children,' she replied wisely. 'I don't want to be involved. If the British offered me the job, I wouldn't take it. I am not a money-lover. I want to serve God. He chose me to be a deaf teacher. I don't need any bribes. I don't accept.'

'Then do us a favour,' he went on. 'Go and tell the people that the 'Japanese' who torture are not Japanese. They are Koreans!' (Koreans were serving in the Japanese Army.)

'I cannot differentiate. We cannot say, "You are Japanese" or "You are Korean". I am Headwoman: the Koreans that I have met come to me with good intentions. How can I say that they are all bad?' Pausing, Ma Ma Hta then said, 'On second thoughts – I will try to mention that the Japanese are kind where I have found them to be so. But it is too late. The Burmese have already formed their opinions of you.'

'The Japanese are good people,' – the *Kempetai* officer maintained. 'Tell them that we are only here to help you Burmese. We are good for you.' He stopped, then used more persuasive words: 'All they have to do is co-operate with us. I will give you a Pass (ticket) – and if you need transport etc. you will be able to have it. You'll be doing good for us as well. To tell good things is your job!'

'To tell good things *is* my job,' (she was thinking in a Christian sense), 'but this appears to me to be bribery – that you want also to offer me a Convenience Pass – which, if I show, the Japanese officers will provide me with whatever I need – such as a car or a bullock cart etc. I don't like that,' she maintained uncompromisingly. 'I don't need any bribes. I will help you for nothing.'

'All right, Ma Ma Hta,' he replied, ending the interrogation.

But the youthful Headwoman had one more thing to say: 'I cannot accept the gifts after all – or I would be like a dog.' The interrogator understood. He smiled and so did she!

Ma Ma Hta was free to leave the room.

After it was all over, Mr Kongo shared with her that the interrogator had told him that he had 'never met a person in Burma with such courage to speak the truth – as that young woman had done'.

Ma Ma Hta knew so often that 'the Lord stood with (her) and strengthened' her (2 Timothy 4:17). She fiercely stresses today that the courage was 'not myself. It was God himself who gave me the courage.' God had said that she was not to be anxious when she was set before the Councils. She was not to think beforehand about what she was to say – because the Holy Spirit would speak through her at the time (Matthew 19: 20). She also says that a certain group of friends and her family were praying for the session.

* * * * *

At Thudawgon, she was welcomed with open arms by all at home. They had been waiting for her (including a group of friends outside - who praised her as she approached the house).

Her father had looked across at his wife and said, 'I told you so!'

Her aunt had said, 'And I told you that she would come back!' – and, smiling broadly, went on – 'And here she is!'

Her mother said to the aunt, proudly and quietly, 'My daughter – she is one who trusts in God.'

They remembered to give *him* all the glory.

* * * * *

In the village of Thudawgon, following the extraordinary visit of the Japanese General, and the arrival of the Headmen, the local people had much to talk about for a long time.

The words that the General had spoken in his speech concerning the wish of the Japanese to be recognised as friends and neighbours, who asked for their co-operation, was probably discussed *ad infinitum*. Although it would seem that those in the Bassein area had suffered very little compared with the Burmese in other parts of the country, there was a deep, underlying spirit of distrust of the Japanese, and secret longings for the day when they would see the last of them. Most had a certain amount of confidence that the British would return, as they had promised.

Ma Ma Hta says: 'We suffered quite a *lot* – but God is good. Whether I was conscious of it or not – at the time – he guided and guarded us. He allows certain uncomfortable things to take place (that we might look to him). Everything is because of God. He is Sovereign Lord. For instance, during the "sword" incident, God was giving me something to show off about the Christian life. I look at things with Christian eyes – I cannot say that *all* Japanese are bad.'

As for local *individual* Japanese officers and soldiers, who may have helped the people, or extended to them unusual friendliness in various ways: well, certain Burmese villagers made increasing allowances for *them* – as 1944 progressed,[1] a year which dragged on uneventfully in their particularly remote district, as regards any military action in Burma.

* * * * *

British RAF aeroplanes were seen intermittently as they flew over the area speeding to intended targets. There were no more bombing raids on Bassein.

One afternoon, as Ma Ma Hta was walking along the main road to the town, she was near two of the bungalows when she suddenly saw a low-flying American Buffalo aircraft slowly heading in her direction just above the bank of the nearest lake! Automatically, she threw herself onto the ground but not before she had seen the two airmen. She glimpsed the face of the pilot distinctly and instantly waved to him!

* * * * *

In the meantime, Ma Ma Hta and her people were unaware that for a large element of the Japanese Imperial Army, the rest of 1944 was a devastating and disastrous period.[2]

In the first place, the British and their Allies had so disrupted enemy communications in Burma that the Japanese had had to make almost superhuman efforts to try to rectify the damage done to their vital links.

Moreover, in the spring, the Japanese had had the temerity to launch a massive invasion into British India – whilst at the same time being unable to guarantee the continuity of the essential provision of military supplies and reinforcements, let alone food, for their obedient troops.

[1.] Note J: January – September 1944
[2.] Note K: April – December 1944: The Japanese

The Japanese had infiltrated through a long section of the border mountains to carry out their attack on NE India. Major Hla Thin, Ma Ma Hta's fiancé , happened to be there just at that time. He had been put in charge of some of the supplies and transport for Burma, in the vicinity of Imphal. By 19th August the last organised Japanese warriors had been forced to leave India in retreat. Their loss of men – through major battles in the Kohima and Imphal regions – was phenomenal.[3]

During the summer the British and Chinese Land Forces, and British and American Air Forces were back, fighting for Burma. The Japanese fought a battle near Mandalay on an enormous scale and lost a large portion of Upper Burma.

By the autumn, the British had supremacy on the ground and in the air throughout the country.

In Rangoon, the Resistance Leader, Aung San, sided positively with the British.

[3.] see Note J

14

Retreat

In Thudawgon, the two doctors were continuing their good work. Some of their patients showed signs of improving, but due to the overall shortage of medicines in Burma, only a small amount of succour could be extended. Any medicines must have been reserved for the military. Nevertheless, the doctors did not desert their dependants. The Burmese, and the Karens, felt increasingly grateful towards them both – especially to the older officer.

Historically, the 'tables appeared to be turning': it was not so much the Burmese who were suffering physically in that part of the country, but the lower-ranking Japanese soldiers. They were obviously very much thinner; many seemed to be listless, some had beri-beri through only eating rice; there was far less available food. But the officers still looked well.

The Burmese people throughout the country must have been weary of war and having to strive continually to find enough to eat.

Naturally a clean, orderly and fun-loving people, now they found it difficult to carry on fairly cheerfully day after day in such a humdrum existence, while at the same time their hearts were weeping for Burma. As a nation they were getting worn down. Ma Ma Hta and many others must have wondered what exactly the British were doing to win back the country. They themselves had to experience suffering, the devastation of their towns, and general mayhem *twice*; 1941–42 and 1944–45. Moreover there was a severe shortage of everything. Their country's plight must have seemed interminable. They wished they could receive news of the outside world. (No helpful British leaflets had been dropped on Bassein as they had been on many other towns.) Wireless sets had been confiscated by the Japanese or hidden by the Burmese. Ma Ma Hta had thrown their radio into the deepest of the three lakes near Kanthonezint as her mother had been over-anxious about it being found in their possession.

* * * * *

Hta Hta herself had been kept free from fears. For example, on the day she was on her way to being interrogated, she says that she 'had nothing' in her mind. 'It was just as it would be if I was walking across the road to see a friend.' Her mind was completely at peace. 'I wasn't afraid of anything. Whenever they asked for me, I had nothing in mind and heart to cause me to be afraid of them. I just wondered why they wanted to see me... God was always guarding us – keeping us from all evils.'

As regards the Japanese suspecting the family of being spies, Ma Ma Hta said, 'Although they knew that we were a Christian family, they also knew that part of our family – one of my brothers and also my brother-in-law – were pro-British and serving with the British Army.

'The Watcher had been planted to spy on us. Whenever I was in Thudawgon I often saw him talking with mother and helping her in the kitchen. My father too spoke with him. He smoked the cheroots that my mother offered to him (made of pounded tree-trunk and leaves mixed with *jagree* and tamarind – thought to be harmless!). He must have found that my parents were friendly.

'One day he asked to see Father – who was surprised when the young soldier apologised to him very sincerely, for spying upon him and his family. He said that the Japanese were thinking wrong about us all. But they had gradually seen and realised that we were good people. He admitted freely to my father that he had done wrong. He said that he was very sorry for watching us continually. He added that he had not done it willingly.

'Much to the young man's relief, my father indicated that he accepted his apology. The Watcher finished by announcing that he was *going*. Just before he went, he solemnly removed all his private belongings out of his hut and presented them to U Chit Htwe and Daw Ma Ma as a gift. We never saw him again.' (No doubt the family gave praise to the Lord believing that he had helped the Japanese soldier to confess his wrongdoing. Ma Ma Hta does not know what her father said to him in his reply.)

* * * * *

One evening, when Ma Ma Hta and her younger brother Baba were staying overnight at Kanthonezint, there was a knock at the door. The Headwoman called 'Who is it?' She was surprised that it was Seito – one of the officers from the *Honjo kikan*. She opened the door (during the day it was always open). He wanted to speak with her.

Ma Ma Hta let Baba know that the officer wished to talk – as a signal that he was to accompany her – so he hurried to change his garment.

In the meanwhile he could see his sister leading Seito to a bench under the trees in the garden. It was a bright, clear, moonlit night and rather chilly for Burma.

Baba joined them. The officer was telling the Headwoman that he was upset that the Americans, who had reacted so strongly after Japan had bombed their ships at Pearl Harbor – which was near the Japanese mainland – were now giving Japan a great deal of trouble. (He had told her triumphantly at the time, that the Japanese had sunk the American Battle Fleet anchored at Pearl Harbor near Honolulu, Hawaii in 1941. The Hawaiian Islands were part of the United States of America.) They spoke for a few more minutes; then Officer Seito suddenly suggested that they sing a couple of hymns together!

Ma Ma Hta – though extremely surprised that he knew any Christian songs of praise, said that she would be delighted to do so. He chose 'Nearer my God to Thee, Nearer to Thee' and 'Love Divine, all loves excelling, Joy of Heaven to earth come down'. He sang in his own language, and she sang the tunes to la-la-lah. Baba remained silent. Before Seito left he asked her to pray for him. She went to bed full of praise to her wonder-working God.

One day the older Japanese doctor came to see Ma Ma Hta's parents. The younger doctor was with him. He was like a member of the family. The children, including Baba, sang and danced for him. 'Then they saw our play.' Before they went, the older man walked outside and laughingly watched the youngsters having a pillow fight – in the creek! Ma Ma Hta said that he was 'obviously happy'.

* * * * *

It wasn't long before everyone knew that the Japanese were moving out of the district;[1] they didn't exactly know why. There were many soldiers passing through the area, going in a northerly direction. But the officers were still in residence.

When the final farewells were to be said, the doctors came through Thudawgon. The older doctor told the family: 'We have to move because of the Allied bombing.' He did not mention the word 'retreat'. Then he said to Ma Ma Hta, 'Will you come and see me off at the station?' Her mother, overhearing him, remonstrated in a low tone: 'No!

[1.] Note L: Second Burma Campaign and Victory: 1944–45

No! No!' She started crying. They walked up towards the house to say goodbye. They then went on towards the station. None of the Japanese looked back. They just continued on, waving once, but looking resolutely ahead.

Ma Ma Hta was holding an exercise book that the older doctor had given her, as she kept her eyes on both of them until they were out of sight. When he had put the book in her hands he had said, 'Don't look at it now. Read it in one or two hours' time.' She had nodded. He had written his home address in it. She knew then that he was retreating. (She never wrote to him; he wrote to the family.) The younger doctor left Ma Ma Hta's brother, Baba, a gift of his fine leather uniform belt. The previous patients had lined the route to see them off.

For the following few days, small groups and platoons of Japanese infantry were passing through the area. They could have been fighting during the months before, in the Arakan, in extremely thick jungle and difficult terrain. Ma Ma Hta says, 'They really were a pitiable sight. They were in a terrible state physically.' They were haggard, exhausted; some had distended stomachs with beri-beri through eating nothing but rice; their uniforms were in tatters and their boots had holes in them. (Many were to die on the way.)

The Burmese Christian community decided to try to relieve the starving young men. They, together with many of the Karens from the nearby village of Thudawlu, made packed lunches for them, each rolled up in a large leaf. 'We looked after them very well.' The women lined the route, passing them food as they struggled along. The emaciated soldiers were of course intensely grateful, some receiving the precious victuals with tears in their eyes. All the women wept openly.

Ma Ma Hta says, 'We did not harbour a grudge against them personally, we just pitied them.' (When the British came back to Burma, though the troops were usually short of rations, they came in with their supplies. And General Slim ordered that a portion of the *Army's* inadequate provisions be used for the *Burmese* in the worst areas of starvation – *Defeat unto Victory*).

Ma Ma Hta says, 'When the doctors had left, mother had wept too. She said that the Japanese were very cruel, but that these Japanese doctors had been very good to us. She told us that she had been really delighted with the doctors. She herself had benefited from their expertise. Then she said, concerning his provision for all the doctors' care – "God is *Good*".'

15

'Peace' in Burma

After the ceasefire in Burma, the family had moved back into Kanthonezint within a week.

A few weeks later some people went up to Rangoon to be with relatives to celebrate Peace, but not Ma Ma Hta's family. 'It was a lovely happy time.' There was a festive atmosphere everywhere in Bassein; joy flowed freely, after all their sufferings. There was a new sense of national unity.

Burma was under temporary British Military Rule. General 'Bill' Slim was in charge of the country. The British Governor had not yet returned to Burma and the Burmese were without an elected Government.

When the time would come for Ma Ma Hta to go back to the Deaf School, she would be surrounded with evidence of war and neglect: debris, rubbish, damaged buildings, roads and water mains. Almost every aspect of administration had been unattended to (some of the key ICS British personnel had been taken away to Japan). Following the war the army brought a certain amount of order into society. In outlying areas of Burma there was immediate famine relief, but in towns inflation was beginning to soar, consumer goods were scarce, there were few cotton goods, and far less food unless on the black market. But gangs of workmen were already clearing rubbish and

rubble, and stopping leakages etc. The military issued a
general newsheet called *The Liberator* – which included
helpful advice, current local and worldwide news, e.g.
that the European war had ended.

On 15th June 1945, Ma Ma Hta and her family went to
see the Victory Parade in Bassein. On the same day in Rangoon, many battle-worn troops were seen lining the route
from early in the morning. Admiral Lord Louis
Mountbatten himself was seen personally pacing out with
military precision the special extensive sections on the
parade ground – for Army, Navy and Air Force servicemen. (Many ordinary Burmese people are said to have felt
'understood' by 'Lord Louis'. Ma Ma Hta and Hla Thin
would experience this on one occasion when they would
meet the South East Asia Command Supreme Commander, in England, years later.)

Admiral Lord Louis Mountbatten was awarded the
highest accolade by the people of Burma – 'Agga Maha
Thiri Thudhama' (the summit of excellence).

* * * * *

The Bassein-based 2nd Karen Rifles, back from the
frontline, asked Ma Ma Hta to find them 'girls' for their
ongoing celebration dances and parties. Parents in
Kanthonezint were less than happy about their attractive,
vulnerable young daughters, some of whom were married, attending such functions – but gave them leave to go,
only if they could get Ma Ma Hta to chaperone them! Her
own father, who didn't approve of these 'goings on' at all,
told her that they must not go without her. She made sure
that there would be military transport for them all and
that they would not be late home. She herself would not
take part in the dancing though asked to do so. 'I do not
like that sort of thing,' she said afterwards.

The parties took the form of a get-together in the evenings. There was music on gramophone records and a

buffet. They were friendly gatherings, with children playing around the room while the community danced. One evening Ma Ma Hta was introduced to Major Neville Hogan (who, in the 1980s and 90s has been interviewed on BBC TV in the UK). He made the following comments in a letter in 1994:

'I was introduced to Ma Ma Hta and her lovely family in August/September 1945 (just after peace with Japan was declared)... Her husband was also a Major in the Army in Burma Reserve of Officers. He too had a distinguished Army career. Ma Ma Hta opened her home to us, fed us, made us welcome and "Happy" with that lovely big smile. She radiated goodwill and Christianity at its best. She asked nothing in return except that we visited as often as we bachelor officers wanted to...'

Major Hogan himself was one of the famous *Chindits*; he also fought in the horrific battle at Kohima, Assam – where only a handful of men had survived.

The War Office, situated at the other side of the three lakes near Kanthonezint, soon let it be known that several secretaries were needed. Ma Ma Hta applied for a job, together with a group of local Burmese Christian girls. As filing clerk she received 250 *Kyats* (*Chetts*) a month, which she considered to be good pay (most of which she saved). She was also able to get free rations, through the military. Every week they gave out tea, coffee, sugar, chocolates and biscuits. Ma Ma Hta's thoughts were with Hla Thin and her brother and brother-in-law, who hadn't yet contacted the family.

Although the mail was not yet back to normal, a letter did arrive from Rangoon, from a Miss Lemon and another missionary, asking her to assist them when they reopened the Deaf School. Her heart leapt; she was thrilled to be

continuing in what she knew to be God's calling for her
and to be with her much-loved deaf children again. She
gave up her job immediately.

Upon her return, she discovered that the building had
been ransacked: 'There was no furniture – nothing.' However, she still had to collect all available pupils – five of
them – and she and the junior Karen teacher did what they
could in the way of educating them. During her off-duty
periods, she would go around Rangoon asking various
people to help the school financially: those in government
and civil service offices; business firms that had supported them in the past and also Burmese Army personnel. She went to the big stores to plead for any necessary
items, such as foodstuffs, paper, exercise books, pencils,
sewing materials and kitchenware. She also went around
to the Rice Distribution Centre, where her young brother
worked, where she collected donations of sugar, salt and
firewood.

Gradually things returned to a semblance of normality
at the school. The number of children was increasing.

One day Ma Ma Hta received a message to say that Hla
Thin, and the other two, were in Upper Burma alive and
well! Folks were travelling from the south to the north and
vice versa, and so it had become possible to send word.

It wasn't long before Hla Thin arrived on the doorstep
at the school. Ma Ma Hta was of course more than
delighted to see him in uniformed flesh, after so long a
separation. They hugged each other, publicly. The children were very excited to see him. Subsequently he came
down to be with Ma Ma Hta about every two weeks.

* * * * *

The familiar Governor of Burma, Sir Reginald Dormand
Smith, returned to Rangoon to a warm welcome by the
mainstream Burmese in the city. He had been the kind of
man that had walked about the town at night, finding out

what the people really thought, by asking them questions in a friendly way.

In April 1947 a General Election was held. It was followed by political unrest in the capital; a certain section of the population was demanding Independence immediately – they wanted a Republic.

British military rule had given way to Direct British Rule, the intention of the UK government being to repair the war damage done to Burma as quickly as possible and then leave the country independent. This was corroborated by a recorded message on BBC Rangoon, given by King George VI. But the nationalists envisaged seeing to the restoration themselves, making use of the available UK Aid package.

After a while a serious illness of the Governor caused his return to England, with the hope that he would come back. In the event, a Major General, Sir Hubert Rance, was appointed Governor instead. However, civil unrest increased, together with hampering strikes.

* * * * *

Ma Ma Hta was conscious of the political troubles in Rangoon. Nevertheless, when she had time she was also collecting things around the town in support of the senior Karen teacher and her few pupils at her home in Henzada – supplying them with parcels 'to keep body and soul together'. When the children had been at Mohnyin in the north, the senior teacher had been in charge; and when the Japanese had laid on trains for people to return home she had travelled alone, taking one or two children to Henzada. Now it would be some time before they would all come down to the Deaf School in Rangoon. Something significant was to happen when they did.

In the meanwhile, the British missionaries, reading 'the signs of the times' foresaw that their days in Burma were numbered. Expecting that Ma Ma Hta would soon be

148 *Ma Ma Hta*

married, they expressed their desire that she and Hla Thin should 'look after the school' when they left the country; Ma Ma Hta would deal with the educational matters and Major Hla Thin with the technical side. The missionaries prayed with Ma Ma Hta about the whole situation. When Hla Thin knew about this, he was agreeable. That was the plan as far as they could see.

But in Burma as a whole, it wouldn't be long before there would be political change. This change would indirectly affect their future lives.

* * * * *

After that first free Election throughout the country, Lord Louis Mountbatten had appointed a young elected politician named Aung San – who was gaining in popularity – to be Leader in the Burmese Government. A point in his favour had been that Aung San apparently preferred Burma to remain within the British Commonwealth of Nations, after Independence.

In the summer of 1947, Ma Ma Hta and her family received some extremely bad personal news.

The news was announced over BBC Rangoon on 19th July: The permanent President, U Nu, and the Executive Council were holding a vitally important meeting about the future Union of Burma, in the old British Secretariat building.

Suddenly, at about 10.30 a.m., a party of gunmen with automatic weapons overcame the guard and swiftly entered the council chamber. They aimed directly at the Chairman, Aung San, and four of his close associates – killing[1] them instantly. Two others were badly wounded.

Ma Ma Hta's younger brother – only in his twenties – who had previously been a jailer in Moulmein, was one of those killed that sad day. She has said very little about the

_____

[1] Information Assassination of Aung San (Maurice Collis).

incident since – only that it was 'because of skulduggery – and foul play'.

U Chit Htwe and Daw Ma Ma's son arranged the funeral in Rangoon. A great number of people came to the service. A well-loved American missionary preached. 'The service was very good.' Before the funeral Ma Ma Hta had advised her mother not to cry – 'as a witness that we are Christians'. Non-Christians often set up a wailing noise. Her mother was very brave; she kept herself under control. In fact, 'nobody cried'.

Ma Ma Hta confessed years later, that when she had advised her mother not to cry, her mother had been very angry. She had said, 'I always thought my mother was dead – but now *you* are my mother!'

* * * * *

On 17th October 1947 there was a Treaty between the British and the Burmese: The Government of the UK recognised the Republic of the Union of Burma as a fully Independent State. This was ratified by the UK Parliament.

Independence Day was celebrated on 4th January 1948 at 4.20 a.m.: 'that moment between the last dusk and early morning and the rising of the sun' in chilly Rangoon. The British flag came down and the Union of Burma flag was raised – it was red with a big white star. The Union was shown by a canton of dark blue surrounded by five smaller stars (see '*Burma*' by N. Bixley). The British left in an atmosphere of goodwill.

'Not all the older generation of Burmese approved of the new regime. A successful businesswoman was heard to ask – "and why are you handing over our country to a bunch of schoolboys who call me Aunty?"' (L. Glass).

Ma Ma Hta says, 'Some of the younger people also were not happy about who was taking over their country.'

* * * * *

By the spring of 1949, most of the ordinary folk in Burma were trying to live as normal a peacetime life as possible. But politically 'practically the whole of Burma was in the hands of some rebel group or other (against their elected government) ... There were clashes between Burmese and Karens.' (L. Glass)

By November, the government was gaining the ascendancy against the dissident groups. But the Karens, who were fighting for a separate, autonomous Karen State that would be in the British Commonwealth and not a Republic, resorted to guerilla tactics.

Ma Ma Hta, busy at the school, and not interested in politics, hardly knew anything about the state of the country – except that there were 'troubles'.

Governor Sir Hubert Rance had appealed to U Nu, the eldest of the young Thakins, to take up the Leadership of the interim government. 'U Nu... brought a character of singular sweetness and a sort of charming naivety into the government of Burma.' (L. Glass) U Nu was an ardent Buddhist, had studied law and was respected by the people.

The government was endeavouring to instil the idea of the new Burma being *Pyidawtha* – a 'sacred, pleasant country' (or 'having peace in the country') – including a Welfare State. Hoarding posters depicted an idyllic kind of 'Castle in the Sky'.

By 1950, Burma began to benefit economically for a period. U Nu chose to introduce the American Marshall Aid programme known as the Colombo Plan. Its main advantage was that, as Burma was virtually bereft of good administrators, money would be provided to help Burmese students and others to be trained abroad in all sorts of useful skills. This scheme was eventually to include Ma Ma Hta and Hla Thin. Ma Ma Hta's family knew U Nu.

* * * * *

They were married in March 1951. Theirs was a quiet wedding, held in the Burmese U Naw Baptist Church in Rangoon. U Naw had been the first convert to Christianity in Rangoon during the previous century.

Ma Ma Hta was sad that her father could not be with them. Babs's father, Mr Raymond, 'gave her away'. The wedding day had been brought forward unexpectedly. This was because Hla Thin's Pastor father wished to marry again; his wife had died. He did not want to remarry before his son had been wed for the first time. The Pastor was no longer physically able and was finding it difficult to carry out his heavy workload – which also involved ministering to several other widely scattered churches in Burma. His preaching and teaching of the Word of God was much in demand.

So Hla Thin married his only love at last!

After a small private reception, the Major had to return to pressing Army duties and his new wife returned to the Deaf School!

The Burmese did not have honeymoons; they went straight into their new home. 'They didn't want to spend a lot of money on one – as they would need it all to start on their married life. Today, some Burmese do have honeymoons like the Westerners!'

Because of the ceremony having been at an inconvenient time, the couple's loyalty and sense of duty had to be paramount. They thought they would soon be working as man and wife at the school.

They trusted the Lord himself to bring them together when *his* time was ripe.

Fun with her relatives, Bangkok, 1998

16

'On Eagles' Wings'

Ma Ma Hta's young husband wrote from his Mandalay base, and then from Akyab Island in the Arakan. She says, 'He wrote all the time, all the time ... love letters.' The same cannot be said of her, in her extremely active life. The number of staff and pupils had increased at the school. The senior Karen teacher had also come down with the children from Henzada. She was not at all happy to hear that Ma Ma Hta and Hla Thin were to take charge of the school, instead of herself.

The influx of returning Burmese, Indians and Chinese business people made Rangoon life seem more normal. Unrest in various parts of the country did not now apply in the city. The new regime happened to remain democratic, at that time.

Yet in the Bassein area there was a big insurrection. Some of the Karens (who were all called Christians), had made a stronghold, with a very good supply of ammunition. When the government's naval forces began shelling their refuge, from the sea, U Chit Htwe decided to take his family to Rangoon to live. He owned a smallish property in the town. So Ma Ma Hta was able to see something of them all. But sadly, Moses, the first born son, who had been Superintendent at the YMCA in Rangoon, died in 1951.

The same year, the Karen people of Burma were finally given their very own State – on the Pegu side of the country. It was named Kayah State but was never self-governing.

* * * * *

On the anniversary of Independence Day, U Nu called for a great co-operative national concert, partly to collect money for the then tiny army led by General Ne Win (Deputy Prime Minister).

Ma Ma Hta was one of the hundreds of women who were to take part. She was to perform in one of the traditional Burmese dances 'to drum music'. Determined to do her best, she danced exquisitely, with the complicated hand movements, revealing a hitherto hidden talent. She happened to be in the front row and caught the eye of U Nu himself. He made enquiries after her, because a government film was about to be made and he needed a suitable actress to take the main part. She was told that it was to be an anti-communist full-length film called *Ludu aung Than* (The Sound of the People's Victory), and she was asked to act in it. She replied that they should ask her husband – which they did. He said, 'Yes, just ask *her.*'

Ma Ma Hta was the 'leading lady' yet she never knew the whole story! The American producer only gave her the simple script for the parts in which she was to play. When it was finished Ma Ma Hta didn't even choose to go and see the film – which was shown all over Burma in the main towns.

In the drama, her husband was a Burmese Communist, who had joined the Party from the army. 'I think he was a Major in the Burma Army. He was an ordinary man. We were already married and had a boy of twelve.' The Producer just explained all the action very simply, referring to his notes. 'We had an ordinary Buddhist family life. When it came to the love scenes, I was supposed to call the husband *Maung* (one meaning is dear, or darling!) Every time that I had to say 'darling' I just couldn't! I kept laughing and laughing! The Director asked why I was laughing. I said: "As soon as I call him *Maung* I want to laugh. Can I address him by his second name?" I was allowed to do that.

'In the film I had to go to the Shwe Dagon Pagoda to pray for my only child. I was supposed to pray before a shrine of Buddha and then bow down to it. When they were filming I went to the cameraman and said, "I am a Christian. Now I have to bow down. I don't want to. I'm a Christian." So he said, "Don't worry, don't worry. There are many camera tricks: You don't have to worry about that at all," he told me; "I'll do that." So he did that for me – so while I was facing like that – facing the Pagoda – in the actual filming I had to turn to *him* – to the camera. He said that I needn't face the shrine at all but to face the camera. At the time I was satisfied with his answer. But later on, my father-in-law wept, because he thought I had done something very wrong and that I should never had allowed myself to pray before a Buddhist shrine. In the film it looked as though I had in fact done so. I had to explain to him what really happened.

'In the story, the husband came back one night with a bloody wound. He looked as if he was dying. I had to cry. Then he died. As I acted I cried real tears. At the end of the scene the Producer said: "Well done, Ma Ma Hta – at the first take – it really touched me." The Director and the cameraman and others were really crying! One said "It's very real."' (It was real because during the scene she had been remembering her own brother, who had been shot – and died. She was actually crying for him.)

* * * * *

1954 – 1956: The 6th Buddhist Synod was held in Rangoon, and administrative inefficiency enabled the military to grow stronger. In 1956 the second elections were held. This time the Opposition Party, the National United Front, had a comfortable majority but the national popular vote was extremely close. It was a 'Caretaker Government'. (*Burma* – Times Travel). Change was on the way.

*   *   *   *   *

'My father and mother were still living in Rangoon with my sisters. In 1954 my dear father died – (went to receive his rewards).

'Mother continued where she was. I was able to see her often. She missed my father so.

'In 1956, on the morning before her death, she said to me, "Last night, your father came and called me. I had the impression that I was going to die." She went to be with the Lord that same day. She had praised God for everything that he had ever given her in life. She told me that he was the One who was supplying her with all his own blessings – to the end.'

*   *   *   *   *

As time went by, a very unusual incident took place at the Deaf School. Ma Ma Hta suddenly found herself in a situation that for a long time she could not understand at all. She was being falsely accused. Jesus her Master had undergone that treatment continually during his ministry. He understood all the reasons.

Miss Lemon was away on furlough in England. The second missionary apparently did not really know the staff very well. She suddenly appointed the senior Karen teacher to be Headmistress, in effect 'deposing' Ma Ma Hta.

It all came about like this. The senior colleague seemed to be jealous of Ma Ma Hta who had been chosen to head the school rather than herself (she had previously enjoyed full responsibility when the children were all in the north in Mohnyin).

One day someone at the Rangoon school let Ma Ma Hta know that she had been suspected of stealing! She could hardly believe it! It so happened that one of the older pupils had been given the minor job of looking after the sewing materials. This girl had informed the senior Karen teacher that Ma Ma Hta had taken a needle and reel of cotton, and had not returned them. Ma Ma Hta taught sewing and had to ask the girl for what she needed.

Nobody had approached Ma Ma Hta about the truth of the matter. 'They kept it to themselves.' The missionary had only asked the young pupil if it was true: she had simply accepted what she had said. 'I was regarded as untrustworthy!' says Ma Ma Hta.

She was extremely hurt and cross about it. But she did not attempt to defend herself. The junior Karen teacher who knew what was going on extended her sympathy by telling her that ever since she had known her she had noticed that she was painstakingly conscientious.

'The whole thing rankled in my mind for a long time.'

Ma Ma Hta went to get advice from a Christian lawyer about the whole situation – after all it involved her husband, who was expecting to work at the school in a post of responsibility. But she says, 'I knew in my heart that it would not be right, as a Christian, to go to court before the unbelievers against my accuser who was Christian, so I took no action.' She allowed herself to be defrauded (1 Corinthians 6:7).

Anyway, the senior Karen teacher, Daw Sein Tha, was designated Headmistress of the well-known Deaf School.

Hla Thin was about to resign, taking early retirement from the Burma Army, in order to help on the technical side of the establishment. Now there was no job for him.

There was, however, to be a completely unexpected development in the offing – God is no man's debtor.

* * * * *

In 1952 all the schools were called State Schools. Major
Thin's resignation did not come into effect. His wife left
the school and went north to live in Maymyo, near Hla
Thin who was in Mandalay. They saw one another at
weekends. Maymyo was a delightful town on the edge of
the Shan plateau, where many servicemen had spent
their furloughs. The newly-weds were there for roughly
one, very happy, year. They were linked with old friends
from many parts of Burma and attended the Baptist
Church where Ma Ma Hta helped, and Hla Thin sang
in the choir and played the piano and his violin. He
had done a little writing – poems, short stories and children's stories, some of which were read over BBC Radio
Rangoon.

Then Major Thin was transferred to Mingaladon, not
far from Rangoon Airport. They lived in a lovely ex-
British bungalow – officers' quarters – with 'a drive, big
shady garden, personal batman, and servants with servants' quarters on the premises', according to Ma Ma Hta.

'While there, we had a communication from Burma's
Leader, U Nu, and the government Arakanese Welfare
Officer (who knew the rest of the family). They had both
decided that we should be recipients of Colombo Plan
Aid. We needed to go abroad to be "trained in the deaf
school world" as teacher of the deaf and technical deaf
aids personnel. U Nu wanted to open up – expand the
whole of the deaf work in Burma. We were to be Heads of
another deaf institution, yet to be opened.'

In the meantime Ma Ma Hta had a lot to do with the
Army Officers' wives at the married quarters. She was
prevailed upon to act as Welfare Officer and was able to do
some very useful social work – helping them with their
personal problems and their children (having 20 of nurs-
ery age on her veranda) and speaking up for the wives to
higher authorities when necessary. She also lent money to

a few reckless young husbands – until pay days! Hla Thin was working at the War Office in Rangoon.

While they were at Mingaladon there was a Resistance Day parade. The weather was blazing hot weather – about 110 degrees. During the course of the proceedings Ma Ma Hta noticed that all the ranks of soldiers, who had marched twelve miles into Rangoon, had been marching about and standing for hours. 'Their faces were red.' Some of them had fainted. There was no water for them. She approached the Commanding Officer, who knew her. She pointed the matter out to him and asked if they could all have a drink. He did not think they needed it: that year the British Army tradition of providing soft drinks had been scrapped, so she requested that *she* could be allowed to contribute and provide drinks for them. He may have been amused at the suggestion, and replied: 'If you can, do it!'. She said, 'I can.' Ma Ma Hta felt that the men were being heartlessly treated. She walked to the superior officer of one unit and asked him to supply an army water tank on wheels, from the depot. She then approached an officer from another unit to provide two sacks of sugar and some limes. She went to where huge blocks of ice were made nearby, and saw that they were smashed up and put into the water tank when it arrived. Then she managed to get a number of enamel mugs from the Recruitment Centre! When the soldiers saw the sugar, lime juice and the ice being put into their drinking water tank they hurried towards it. In the end they had all slaked their thirst – and lay on the ground exhausted but blissfully happy! Ma Ma Hta's military husband was concerned about what some of the senior officers would make of her action. She told him that if something came of it *she* 'would stand for it' – he needn't worry.

* * * * *

In 1958 came the very sad news that Ma Ma Hta's younger brother, Baba, had also died. He had helped her during their days at Kanthonezint and Thudawgon.

The couple had been transferred to Thaton, then Moulmein in 1958. There Major Thin found that he was being discriminated against – in favour of very young soldiers with little experience. He did not complain. He never asked for anything. He took it all patiently and humbly, though with proper dignity. He was being pressured (because he had been in the *British* Army). Other youngsters were promoted before him. 'A junior officer was given a jeep; he could have a small van.' He was given a 'Refresher Course' – with very young soldiers (officers); it was an Assault Course. Army visitors from abroad asked him to be an interpreter. He was also sent into very real danger zones on many night patrols, whereas the younger men were often spared the same. His wife was afraid that he would be killed. It seemed as if the devil was aiming to get rid of both of them at this time '... seeking whom he may devour' (1 Peter 5:8).

Ma Ma Hta was *also* in danger one day. She went on a boating picnic to Mergui and Tavoy with some of the army wives. As they were about to round a headland, stormy waves almost capsized the fairly large boat. She sent up a quick prayer to her heavenly Father and a big wave undergirded the vessel and carried it smoothly round the point. She was able to give a Christian witness to the young women, while they were picnicking on the beach.

* * * * *

Towards the end of 1958, Major Hla Thin took early retirement from the Burma Army and was on an army pension. The following year they went back to Rangoon and thence to Maymyo Hill Station, living in the vacant house of a relation. They were waiting for a Colombo Plan Grant and also a passport, to leave the country for the UK where they were to begin their training; but they had not envisaged staying there for about one and a half years! However they were extremely happy in Maymyo.

One of Ma Ma Hta's favourite spiritual songs, which she sang quite often at that time, was:

> I'll go where You want me to go, dear Lord,
> I'll be what You want me to be,
> I'll say what You want me to say, dear Lord,
> I'll be what You want me to be.
> It may not be on the mountainside
> Or over the deep blue sea – but
> > [repeat the first four lines]
> > > (Based on C.E. Rounsfell's original words)

It wasn't until September 1961 that Ma Ma Hta and Hla Thin left their homeland by air, bound for England.

They had been hindered in several ways – 'But God' – who causes his people to be men after 'his own heart'; who blessed shepherd David, son of Jesse with his gifts of 'integrity of heart and skilfulness of his hands'; and had chosen and guided him to feed and lead the sheep of Judah: this very same God, was about to lovingly separate and guide Ma Ma Hta and her husband to the particular *locations* of the work to which He (alone) had called them (Psalm 78:72, Acts 13:2).

Gift for the School for the Deaf, Rangoon, 1990s

17

England

'My very first teaching experience abroad, out of my country, was in England in 1961. In September 1961 the Burmese government wanted Hla Thin and myself to go to the UK under the Colombo Plan.

'The Colombo Plan meant that my husband and I were sent to Exeter Royal School for the Deaf, which is one of the biggest schools in England. We were there six weeks, partly to become acclimatised. We thank God for the Colombo Plan. We thoroughly enjoyed ourselves there; and were also taken by car on interesting trips through Devon and Cornwall to see the beautiful countryside. We were also taken to Spastics, Mental and Handicapped Institutions. At Exeter, the Headmaster, Mr Kettlewell, and his wife looked after us very well. I am very grateful to them.' (He realised that Ma Ma Hta had a special rapport with the children and immediately allowed her to do some of the teaching.) 'It was a residential school with about 250–300 pupils; whereas the one in Burma only catered for 50–60. This school was also very modern – with gadgets, apparatus and deaf aids. Nevertheless, our missionary headmistress in *Rangoon* once said, "Hta Hta, in this school the children are doing very well."

'In the 1960s in the UK the behaviour of the English pupils was good, but as the years went by they began to misbehave more at home. I know all children can be naughty at times in school, but not so in Burma – they're afraid of the teachers. We can control them in the schools. Even if I taught as many as ten *deaf* pupils, I could manage them.

'We had problems in actually educating the deaf – but behavioural problems, no. I only experienced them in *this* country: it is just because, here, the children have everything.

'After six weeks we left Exeter; we were sent up country to Doncaster, via London, where we stopped off to visit more schools for the deaf. Having left all our luggage in a hotel until noon, we went back to find that we had lost all our worldly goods, including Burmese clothes, my jewellery, and my big *Judson English Dictionary* which I used to read the Bible in English. Some time later we were advised to write to the hotel and claim compensation. Writing down the original price of each item instead of the then going rate, people told me that I was "silly"! I thought I was simply listing the actual value.'

In Doncaster they went to the large Yorkshire School for the Deaf. Ma Ma Hta was to live in one of the small flats set aside for staff. Hla Thin returned to London because he was to take a comprehensive one-year course at the University of London in Malet Street, to be a fully qualified Deaf Aids Technician. He lived in one room in Gower Street. Once again, they were to be separated most of the time, except when she travelled to London to be with him for a few weekends, or during holiday periods. When she joined him, the landlord did not charge Hla Thin any extra rent, which helped considerably. Ma Ma Hta was at the Doncaster School from October 1961 to April 1965.

'In Doncaster I had very useful teaching experiences and was grateful to the Headmaster, Mr Greenaway, and the staff who were most helpful in all respects. It was great. I had a class of six boys and girls from 5 to 8 years of age. They loved me and I loved them – very nice children.

'There was an inter-schools Writing Competition – the deaf children included. I was pleased and proud of my pupils' results, especially as one of my girls won Second Prize. It was a great achievement.'

Ma Ma Hta was a lively teacher and thoroughly enjoyed the children. The staff had some good laughs out of her, especially when she found everything so strange in England compared to what she was used to. She was not hurt and always laughed *with* them. Once, during the winter, she asked why the English didn't cut down all the 'dead trees' (the ones without leaves) – because in Burma all the trees were green all the year round, only shedding a few leaves at a time. Another time she was confused because when she was feeling 'run down' she was advised to go and buy some 'Guinness' (ale) to take as a tonic. She amused the chemist when she asked for it (she had gone to naturalist chemists when she needed a 'pick-me-up' in Burma). She thought she would have to go into a public house and didn't want to enter one. Then she had to learn that it was available in a shop not a 'pub'.

She has a delightful sense of fun. 'I'm not very good at English, but I do get "results" in the speech and understanding – of the deaf pupils.' As time went by, a boy named Keith Wood had a misunderstanding of a word: 'I was teaching about the weather. When it snowed I wrote "It is snowing" on the board. All were keen to tell it to me. The same applied to rain, hail, fog etc. I said that when it is foggy you can't see *through*. Keith came to me on a bright sunny day, showed me his Wellington boots – pointed to his name written inside them, and said, "It's foggy!" I asked him what he meant. "Yes, it's foggy – you can't see through – look." I could see that his name was almost illegible: "Look, it's rubbed out – it is foggy." I told Mrs

Newbonne, a colleague, that Keith thought that "foggy" meant that you can't see properly. We all three laughed. She said that I was clever, and so was Keith. I said that *he* was the clever one because he linked it with the fact that you "couldn't see clearly" '.

Ma Ma Hta had no idea what to make her class perform for the Christmas Concert. Then she remembered the children's chorus:

Jesus died for all the children
All the children of the World -
Red and yellow, black and white
All are precious in His sight;
Jesus died for all the children of the World.

'Each child was dressed in some National Costume. I put a revolving globe on stage, then asked: "Where do *you* come from?" The child answered – say – "China". Then he/she would have to go and point to it on the globe. Our item was a great success. Everybody clapped and clapped.'

* * * * *

In 1962 Hla Thin and Ma Ma Hta managed to get Ann (her cousin whom she had adopted) and Babs into England for training. They hoped to work later as a team, in a deaf school in Burma. Babs would be a teacher and Ann would help with sewing classes on the domestic side. They had two single rooms at the Doncaster School.

Ma Ma Hta was on half the wages of the rest of the staff as she had no work permit. 'I didn't mind how little I got. God supplied me. We weren't hungry: we even saved money.'

Ma Ma Hta began to be concerned that she was receiving 'double wages' and began to send back the £49 monthly Colombo Plan money. 'When I told the Bursar at the school the reason why I wanted to withdraw my £49, he tried to get me to change my mind! He asked for a letter from my husband to verify that I wanted to give it up. He added that I'm working so I *should* take the money from the school, anyway. I replied that the Colombo Plan money could be used for somebody else instead. The Plan people wrote to thank me for my offer and my honesty. They said that they hadn't ever had anyone returning money, since the start of their aid programme (which included people from other nations). They said that everyone earned wages. They had decided to send me money for all my holidays – which my pay didn't cover.'

Hla Thin eventually moved to Doncaster and Mr Greenaway, who was also a Hearing Aids Technician, let him gain experience at the school. He was not paid. Hla Thin wrote a play for children. It was accepted by the BBC for radio, for which he was paid £200. The BBC interviewed us, on air, because they wanted to report on the Colombo Plan. 'They were pleased with all of us Burmese. I had my happiest time in England, at that school.'

Because the entire school building had to be vacated during each school holiday, and it became expensive to go with Ann and Babs down to London and hire two double rooms regularly (though the landlord didn't make her pay for *her* double) she decided to buy a cheap two bedroomed house in Doncaster – so that they could all be together during holidays. Hla Thin had passed his examinations with flying colours and was given a job as an apprentice at St Mary Abbott's Hospital in Kensington for a time. He got a £50 London Allowance.

* * * * *

A handsome intellectual man from Sri Lanka, named Norman Martinesz, suddenly appeared on the scene to see Babs, who by now had become a really beautiful and charming young woman. They had first met when they had been at University in Poona. Norman and a friend had come to England to join the Royal Navy. He had asked Babs to marry him, while they were in India.

'When he was in the Navy at Gosport, Babs asked us if she could become engaged. We, as seniors on the spot, gave our permission. Her mother, in Rangoon, was happy about it,' says Ma Ma Hta.

* * * * *

Ma Ma Hta writes: 'I would like to digress and write about the teaching of the deaf in general. I want you to know that the deaf are very difficult to teach in order that they may understand and communicate. One would think that this would be fairly normal. But think – the child has not been able to hear since the day that he was born. Comparing him with a blind child, the blind may be better off. The blind receive more sympathy, but when you consider it – it's just that they cannot see (which is terrible). However, they can say, they can ask – what, where, when, why and so on. They can express their feelings and what not. From an early age they can hear conversation, learn to talk and understand many things.

'As an example: I was taking a doctor's child back home on holiday on the ferry. Suddenly the man beside him asked, "Do you know what time it leaves?" Of course there was no answer. The man asked again, with the same result. Then he remarked, "What's the matter with you? Didn't you hear me?" Interrupting, I explained that the boy was deaf. "What! Deaf?" "Yes, he does not hear you." I explained about it. At that time many people had never heard of the deaf. In some ways the deaf are more unfortunate than the blind.

'Because of experience with teaching of the deaf over many years, I had learnt to assess whether a child *could* be taught in the first place or not, as do many people who happen to be the pioneers, or advocating research concerning the deaf. They are doing very well in their field but, as for myself, for years I had no instruments with which to test the children – but we can at least, by long experience, assess whether a child is teachable or not. It is something anybody can say. It is love, or a gift or a talent also; I do not know what to say. I am not highly educated or holding degrees. Simple intuition tells me whether a pupil is capable of assimilating speech.

'For example: The Head of the Assessment Department says that two of my deaf children are not eligible for teaching – because they are *multi-handicapped*. Right – now I am nobody to comment – but in my mind the two children are mentally normal. In one school my class was a multi-handicapped and deaf class. That means that many deaf schools are just for the normally deaf: a single teacher can have four to eight children if the children are partially deaf and can use hearing aids or some other kind of gadget.

'But, it is doubly difficult for the deaf-*handicapped* pupils. I had *ten* deaf children in my class: no helper, no assistant, no hearing aids and what not. All right, I taught them by the oral method – an old type of teaching speech and lip reading.

'Two other true stories as an example: one of my boys was an intelligent one. I was teaching them, as my other colleagues did, with wallcharts – of nouns, verbs, names etc. One day I was teaching tenses: present and past from a chart. First, I asked them to jump, run, sit, hop and fall; they enjoyed that. When they stopped I said "Good. It is finished." So on the backboard I wrote the words: jump-jump*ed*, run-ran, sit-sat, hop-hopp*ed*, and fall-fell. I said: "It is past tense, so you have to *add ed*. This one has become jump*ed*. When the word hop comes, you have to add *-ped*." "Why not -ed again?" the boy asked. I answered: "If a *vowel* is in front of a consonant you have to add two p's." Then this boy showed me why I do not add two p's for jumped! He said that the same applied to the reason why we had to used two p's in hopped! He understood my explanation. He had a good brain.

'The second incident was when I was teaching numbers 1–10, 11–20, 21–30 and so on. "Why isn't eleven *ten*-ty one, instead of eleven? Like *twenty*-one, *thirty*-one etc."

'I hesitated. If I could not explain he would sign the teacher off as stupid! Then – sudden inspiration came to me – "When the children become teenaged, 13–19, the boys are addressed as Master," I said. "When they are 20–21 they're called Mister. When a boy is 20 we do not say 'teen. There is no more eleven, twelve, thirteen etc." He accepted that.

'The third incident was when teaching how to read Roman numerals which were on some of the school clocks. A different boy, Robert, was there. I started by counting 10–1 backwards. "The Romans were clever," I told the class. "Now, watch very carefully. Our numbers are 10,9,8,7,6,5,4,3,2,1. Roman numbers are X,IX,VIII, VII,VI,V,IV,III,II,I – All right?" Robert came to the backboard, pointed out the numbers and said, "I can understand I,II,III,IV,V,VI,VII,VIII,IX,X, but I cannot understand why IV=4 and IX=9." I explained: "5–1=4=IV (minus one on the *wrong side* of V), and so 10–1=9=IX." "Yes, I now understand. But why isn't 10=X written with 2 V's?"

'I was very pleased with his questions and his logic. I had to answer to his satisfaction. Instead of his 2 V's I showed him V up and V down = an X (by crooking my two forefingers, one up and the other down, placing one directly on top of the other, forming an X). He was delighted with my illustration. He was fired to show off his ability; he continued writing the Roman numerals up to XXX, then he stopped and said that he preferred our numbers, and that the Roman ones were difficult to remember. He said that he could now read the clock with Roman figures for numbers.

'Robert "made" that day for both of us.

'It was the day that I thanked God for making me successful in my aim to make the so-called multi-handicapped deaf children become "normal deaf". He gave me the talents, patience and love. He fulfilled my aim. There was no earthly reward, nothing. Nobody knew what great things *he* had done.

'Altogether two to five of my multi-handicapped deaf pupils were proven normal, and were accepted by the Normal Deaf Department and promoted.'

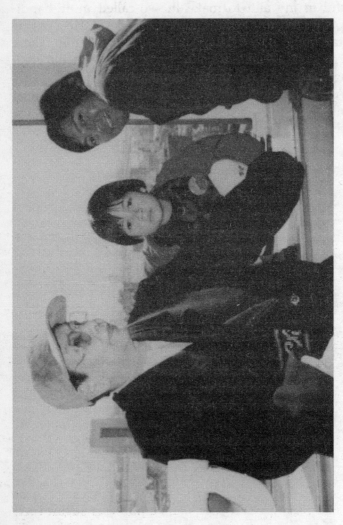

Sightseeing with relations, Tokyo, 1997

18

'This is the way – walk ye in it'

In 1965 – the Colombo Plan courses and experience came to an end. Major Hla Thin and Ma Ma Hta returned to Burma (now renamed Myanmar). The country was under an army regime headed by General Ne Win.

'We lived in Rangoon. It was a great joy to be back amongst our relations and friends. Having relinquished our passports, we were asked to write reports on our UK training. We did not hear anything from the government about the jobs promised by U Nu, who was no longer in power.

'We now found that we had much difficulty in obtaining necessary food. My husband was on a Burma Army pension. There was a black market for those with money. Only the military and the top people were able to get the best rice. Everyone had ration tickets for a measure of inferior rice, a bottle of oil, and salt – but no garlic or chillies etc. We hadn't been told that we had to have coupons. At the distribution point for our district I said that my husband was an ex-serviceman and that I needed rice. Normally I should have got a bag of rice, two tins of evaporated milk and some sugar. I had noticed that a family of five had been given a very small amount of sugar: I felt very unhappy about them.

'Whatever the government had planned – things were obviously not working out in practice; there was corruption. As I stood before the distributor that day, some army officers came in and walked to the front of the queue, and took everything! (One was even a Major from the wrong district.) I then went along to the firing range where (I had just been told) I could obtain a coupon for my husband. The man there said that only *active* service personnel could *pay* for one. I replied that we really needed it. He said, "Then I will give it." Although we were in need, I stated that I had to go according to the rules. If I must have a ticket, he needn't worry, I would get one. He'd see – I would come back.

'It so happened that the same evening a man at "The People's Shop" was distributing his meagre supply. There were one hundred people but he only had enough for sixty of us. He said that he had a "Bran Tub" in which he had concealed sixty food items; I was able to get at least one item. The last forty got nothing. The Lord blessed us because my army brother-in-law was able to give us some provisions.'

The couple went up to Maymyo hill station where the situation was better. They received another letter from the government asking them to send a report on their Colombo Plan UK training. So they rewrote the whole thing and posted it to them for the second time. They heard nothing about any jobs in a school for the deaf.

While at the Doncaster Deaf School, the Head – Mr Greenaway – had suggested that they apply for work in a College for the Deaf in Massachusetts, USA. He had written recommendations. They waited over a year for the Burmese government to move but heard no more from them – 'So we decided: all right we'll go to the USA. We applied and were accepted by the Massachusetts College. We bought our air tickets. We applied for passports, but they did not come. We went to see the authorities in Rangoon: we showed them our credentials and correspondence with the Americans, together with a visa from the USA. They said that if we wanted to go to America we could go. We were sent our passports, but too late – the College people wrote to say that they could no longer hold the posts open for us, after waiting for six months. Also, the British Embassy official told us that if we still wished to try for work in the United States, we could fly via the UK and *could* get "transit" there. We hoped to see Ann, Babs and Norman. In March 1967 we took a flight to the UK.'

* * * * *

When they arrived at London Airport, Ma Ma Hta 'was really very angry' with the officials. They did not give permission for them to stay, even for transit. 'We were questioned and had to prove that what we said was true, and had to show our application to the American College – and all our credentials. They should have known that we were all right. When we told them about Hla Thin's service in the *British* Army during the 1939–45 war, one official remarked "That is past history." Anyway, they did allow us transit, for a while.'

Major Hla Thin couldn't forget the inference of his hazardous service being simply 'past history'. During the SOE Missions he and his colleagues had frequently been in danger of their lives – for Britain.

Although they had transit, they had very little money but were assisted by a few sympathetic English people who put them in touch with those who could help them financially in a small way, as they were without work permits. A veteran of the Burma campaigns gave Hla Thin the opportunity, as an apprentice, to acquire a skill of lithography in his metal workshop. He employed only British soldiers who had been in Burma. It was a perfect job for Major Thin with his artistic talents and to be working amongst men who liked Burmese people. Through the

Royal Association for the Deaf, Ma Ma Hta was able to give private tuition to two deaf girls, one of whom had a French mother. Once Ma Ma Hta took that particular child on an outing to Southsea. She unwittingly showed the girl over 'HMS Victory' – Admiral Nelson's ship – which led the English fleet to victory against the French and their Spanish allies, at the Battle of Trafalgar. The girl's mother was not pleased with Ma Ma Hta!

Hla Thin and his wife applied for vacancies at the Royal School for the Deaf in Margate, but were not accepted because they did not possess work permits. At that time Hla Thin's employer decided to contact the ex-Governor of Burma, Sir Hubert Rance, to see if he could do anything for him. It so happened that Sir Hubert was about to retire from the Home Office. He approached Admiral Lord Louis Mountbatten to see if he could help Major Thin. Ma Ma Hta and her husband were invited to see Admiral Lord Louis Mountbatten. (Ma Ma Hta was not happy about being 'spoken for'. She says: 'Hla Thin knew all about that. I had nothing to do with it.') However, they found the illustrious Commander of South East Asia Command to be very understanding. Not long afterwards they received a personal letter from the great man informing them that they had been granted permits to live and work in the United Kingdom. They were grateful to him.

So it was, that the Lord showed them that *this* was the way in which they were to walk. He had clearly guided them by shutting the door to work in America and setting before them an open door in Great Britain.

Ma Ma Hta says, '1967 proved to be a very dark year – a hard time for us.' It wasn't so much a matter of finding it difficult to settle; they had weathered changes before. It was the fact that they were living on extremely little money. Since the war, Ma Ma Hta and her family had lost all their belongings, including their entire home. (Once she had returned to Kanthonezint to discover that there was *nothing* left in their house – 'not even a needle'.) Now they were having to start from scratch. Major Thin was at least receiving a small British Army pension. Their jobs brought in a mere pittance. They rented a room not far from Wandsworth Common, South London. At times Ma Ma Hta had to baby-sit for the landlady's children – to help make ends meet. Eventually they decided to sell the Doncaster house which Norman, Babs and Ann had been using. All three moved down to a house in Gosport.

In 1969 they re-applied to the Royal School for the Deaf, Margate. This time they had success. On 2nd June they joined the staff and were accommodated in an upstairs flat next door to the school, which overlooked the extensive grassy grounds of a building which ressembled a red brick mansion.

The Headmaster, Mr Pursglove, did his best to make the two 'foreigners' welcome. Ma Ma Hta's glowing recommendation from the Doncaster Head must have helped her to be given a class of six boys and girls who were not only deaf but *multi-handicapped* as well. It was a great test of endurance for her. She says that she had to watch each individual all the time – to see that they came to no harm. However she prayed much, and taught them as much as they were able to imbibe. As previously mentioned, a couple of them had very good brains and through her assistance were put into the Normal Deaf Department.

In course of conversation with Mr Pursglove they found that he had been a prisoner of war under the Japanese and had been forced, with hundreds of other soldiers, to build the famous northern-Siam (Thailand) railway line which went right through into Burma. Part of the track ran along sections that had once been solid rock. Sometimes they had even taken to eating *grass* to try to alleviate their gnawing hunger. He had seen hundreds die of exhaustion, malnutrition, cruel treatment and disease. When the Burmese couple were speaking of the Japanese, the Head said, 'Please don't talk about them; I don't want to hear.' They understood why.

Ma Ma Hta brought some fun and laughter into the staffroom at the school. Her way with children was remarkable; there was always something interesting taking place during her lessons. Whenever visitors from other places, including America, came to see the school they were always shown into her classroom in particular to watch the children at work. One day, a collecting box for some good cause was passed round to all the staff. Ma Ma Hta happened to have put in a £10 note. The Head took it as possible that she was pulling their legs or a case of not having had enough change. She said that she thought that those people's need was much greater than hers.

The following is a testimonial kindly sent by two of her colleagues at the Margate School:

What we remember about Mrs Thin

Mrs Thin was a very kind lady.

She was a strict disciplinarian who ruled her class firmly but fairly. Although she was strict she was flexible and understanding, and the best interests of the children were always her main concern.

Mrs Thin was hard-working, honest, reliable and utterly trustworthy. She was a devout Christian who worshipped regularly at Cecil Square Baptist Church, Margate. Her Christian beliefs and principles shone through in her life. She was always willing to help other people in whatever way she could. She was a modest and self-effacing lady, who never sought the limelight.

Mrs Thin had a stable and happy family life. While Mrs Thin taught at the RSDC Margate, her husband was, for a number of years, the school's Audio-Technician. Her daughter, Ann, was a member of the school's Childcare Staff and worked with primary age children. In later years, Mrs Thin helped to nurse Ann through a painful and long drawn-out illness, until Ann's death from cancer in 1989...

Mrs Thin kept in close contact with family members both in Britain and in Burma. Her family was very important to her. Mrs Thin had a multitude of friends. When she retired from teaching she spent a lot of time at her house in London, and her London home was always open house to any Burmese people, students, friends or acquaintances, who were studying, working and living in this country. Being in London and having regular contact with Burmese people, made her, she said, feel closer to her own country. Mrs Thin loved her native land as she remembered it, and she always wore Burmese dress. She was always happy to impart knowledge of her homeland to others.

We remember Mrs Thin as a quiet, dignified and much-respected colleague, friend and neighbour. She was always willing to reach out the hand of friendship to anyone. She was a very hospitable lady, and we were made welcome in her home whenever we cared to call.

P.M. GALLAGHER and B. GJERNES

Babs and Norman now resided in a lovely house in Alverstoke. He had an important job in Environmental Health in Southampton. They had a daughter, Kay, who was heading for university. In the 1970s Ann came to work at the school in Margate. She bought a small house nearby.

Mr and Mrs Thin had purchased the South London house. She began decorating it herself, and did what she could with the garden. It was presently occupied by a succession of Burmese tenants – doctors doing further studies and students on courses. They still kept their own room as a base as they looked forward to their retirement. She and Hla Thin lived frugally and very simply. They were always distributing to the necessity of the saints (in Burma); and given to hospitality at home. The plight of the church in Burma was ever on her heart. Whenever possible Ma Ma Hta was supporting needy church members in *Burma*; prices were high and there were many who couldn't get jobs. She had also bought a Retirement Home for church workers in Rangoon.

* * * * *

Major Hla Thin retired in July 1980 – after giving invaluable service, not the least towards the hundreds of children who passed through the school, and who enjoyed his warm, loving personality, his fun and his teasing!

Ma Ma Hta retired in December the same year. They moved to their home in London. They invited the author, among many others, to their unadorned middle floor flat.

1981 was the year in which General Ne Win retired from the Presidency. He retained political control as *Chairman* of the 'Burma Socialist Program Party' which was the sole legal one. (*Burma* – Times Library).

A few years before, Mr and Mrs Thin had become British citizens. It must have been hard for them to do so, for their hearts would naturally ever be rooted in Burma. They were grateful to this country for having them.

Ma Ma Hta went on the first of her long-distance travels, while at Margate. She and her husband were invited to the USA for the Burma Star Association Reunion held in a 5-star hotel in Washington DC. About six hundred people attended. When they had a big party, they asked Hla Thin to sing. 'He sang a lot of songs, leading the show in a singsong of wartime tunes.' Then they wanted Ma Ma Hta to give them a song. She told them she couldn't sing, but when they insisted, she sang: 'Which came first? – the chicken or the egg - the egg or the chicken – the chicken or the egg?' which set them off roaring with laughter!

Major Hla Thin and his wife were very happy to stay on for two months, with a nephew of General Sir William Slim whilst in America. 'Hla Thin knew the General.'

* * * * *

By now both Ma Ma Hta and her husband had heart trouble; but Ma Ma Hta's seemed gradually to right itself, later on. There was to be a Margate Burma Star Reunion. The couple had always gone down from London together for it. Hla Thin had to go in advance – to prepare things, but this time, because they were putting up a sick Pakistani lady and her little girl for a few days, Ma Ma Hta felt that she couldn't leave them. She accompanied Hla Thin to the coach station. While he was waiting in the coach to depart, she had a strange 'kind of premonition' as she looked at him. 'My heart suddenly went out to him. I felt so sad that he had to go without me – so very sad as I looked at him. I was really sorry that I couldn't go with him.' The coach started – and he was gone.

Ma Ma Hta had told Hla Thin that she would follow on the Thursday. He surprised her by phoning to say that he would come back on Sunday. He said: 'Stay there; and when I come back will you please dye your hair (black) – because we're going to a special Association dinner at the Royal Albert Hall!' She was pleased that they would at least travel down on the Thursday – together.

But on 18th March 1987 Major Hla Thin was on the way back to his hotel after having dined elsewhere, when he had a major heart attack. By the time he had been rushed to hospital and into Intensive Care, he suffered a massive coronary – and suddenly died.

His dear wife couldn't forgive herself that she had let him go alone. She was so grieved that she had not been with him when he most needed her. She remembered that she had not even said 'Goodbye'. She was reminded that he had told her about a dream that he had had – almost a month beforehand. Why hadn't she recognised it as, maybe, a warning. The thoughts went round and round in her tortured mind. He had told her that in his dream he was having a nice bath. Then he dreamt that met an old non-Christian friend and he knew in his heart that the day for his own death was getting nearer and nearer. Two or three times he was going towards the church when he met someone on the way. One person that he saw was a man with a very, very old violin which had a sound that was not good. He asked, 'Can I have your violin?' When *he* played it, he played and played. He had never had such a violin – it had a marvellous sound!

The funeral of Major Hla Thin was held in Margate. 'He was given full military honours – with a military escort, and the British 'Union Jack' flag draped over his coffin. It was a big funeral; a lot of people were there. We had a service at the Baptist Church which was full; and after that a very nice service at the crematorium, where the chapel was filled with many who hadn't been able to get to the church. During both services, men of the Burma Star Association, as well as the British Legion, spoke highly of Hla Thin.'

Not long after her husband's death, Babs and Norman asked Ma Ma Hta to come and live with them.

Ma Ma Hta felt she should stay in London a while longer. Ann had developed cancer and came to spend the rest of her days with her. On 1st April 1989, when she also died,

Ma Ma Hta realised that she had been impressed by the fact that Ann had never once complained, in all her agony. Right at the end she was thinking of Ma Ma Hta. She said 'Never mind, Mother' – and passed into the presence of her Lord.

* * * * *

Ma Ma Hta had many relations – particularly those of the younger generation. They lived in Burma, Thailand, Japan, Australia and California, USA. She had invitations to go and see them – or rather they wanted to see *her*. Ma Ma Hta understands young people. When Ma Ma Hta visited Japan, her relations traced the whereabouts of the son of the older Japanese doctor, who had given voluntary medical aid to the Burmese in Thudawgon during the War. She was able to meet his son who told her that his father had died of natural causes. He himself was now in charge of his father's private hospital. Ma Ma Hta was glad to be able to tell him of the older doctor's concern for her people, for which they were intensely grateful.

She also learnt that Seito, the *Kempetai* officer, had also died in the intervening years.

After she had gone to live with Babs in Alverstoke, she travelled to all those countries, except Australia, and also to Switzerland and Sri Lanka (about four times) because Norman and Babs had another house in Kandy.

Babs went with Mrs Thin the last time she went to Burma. They stayed with Babs's mother – Ma Ma Hta's last remaining sister – who was an influential Seventh Day Adventist.

Ma Ma Hta stayed on in Burma after Babs had returned home. She is grateful to the Government of Myanmar that they allowed her back as she is a citizen of the UK. Due to extreme heat – and the fact that the electricity was 'rationed' and there were times when fans and refrigerators ceased to function, she became ill. Ma Ma Hta longed to settle down and end her days in Rangoon. However, because of certain unforeseen occurrences she knew that she ought to give Babs's *mother* the little house that she had just bought for herself there; and she returned to England and Alverstoke.

Epilogue 1998

Ma Ma Hta is still in Alverstoke, with Babs.

The first time that the author visited her there, she was sitting on the floor in the reception room, carefully combing the Alsatian dog's hairs out of the whole carpet!

There are certain things which Ma Ma Hta finds difficult in her latter years. The continual underlying one is the great loss of Hla Thin. Another is daily learning to sit still, having led such an active life, and now being in the position of having very little to do – as she is so well loved and looked after. She used to enjoy walking the dog to the beach in the early morning, to keep it from disturbing the others. But it died. Anyway she often prepares the vegetables for meals, waters the peaceful garden and tries to keep busy with small jobs. At the same time she still bubbles with joy and laughs easily!

When on her own in London she had regularly walked across Wandsworth Common in the early morning to do physical exercises. Now that she is frail and feels rather weak she finds it hard to accept that she is losing her accustomed strength. She performs simple exercises and massages her own aching bones, fairly successfully. Yet she knows that 'When I am weak, then am I strong' spiritually (2 Corinthians 12:10) and that 'though our outward man perish yet the inward man is renewed (in spirit) day by day' (2 Corinthians 4:16).

In London she used to pin a list on the wall above her bed – which showed her the days and times of every weekly religious programme available on radio and television. She listened to or watched as many as she could, hoping to glean spiritual life from them; and she joined in with the Worship Service each morning at 10 a.m. on BBC Radio 4.

But the main part of each day is spent in reading the Bible, praising God and praying. The last time the author was with Ma Ma Hta she told her that she is searching the Scriptures to see what God *really* says, and also, to *learn* – so that she might be able to answer the people who don't know him; and be able to meet their spiritual need.

Norman, Babs, their daughter Kay and her husband David are very hospitable. Friends and visitors are welcomed most warmly – at any time of day or night. People often pop in for a chat and stay for hours! Also, there is always at least one young male student living in as 'family'. Ma Ma Hta's quiet influence has meant that at least one is now reading and studying the Bible privately because he wants to. Day by day general conversation with anyone who happens to be in the house at any time is invariably intercepted by Mrs Thin's apt, loving yet piercing spiritual comments, stated with neither fear nor favour. They all love and respect dear Ma Ma Hta – 'Kyee Kyee' (*Chee Chee*), Great Auntie.

Her prayers these days are first and foremost for her entire scattered family – and for all Burmese people – and also for all others throughout the world, who are not yet reconciled to God their Creator.

When Ma Ma Hta was asked what she wanted to *say* in the book about her life – she replied: 'I want it to be known that God always had the most marvellous plans. There were many times when I had no idea what he was doing with me.

'As I look back – I say, God is great! Even if there were dangers that I didn't know about – he always stopped things from happening to me, like being arrested at Bassein Hospital.

'We must *thank* God. He really is love. He knows who is who. He looks after everybody and does what is best for us according to his own will and purpose – that we might be changed, to be like his Son...

'I am eighty-five – I have no house of my own: I have no children of my own. Therefore I can help other people. The thing is – God let me *have* – so that I can contribute or give away things in this world.

'As long as I live, he looks after me: I don't need to worry. I mean exactly that; I don't need or worry about anything. The food I eat is very simple and it is good. At the place where I live – I'm very pleased to say – all will care for me. In all places – wherever I go – my relations and friends continue to look after me.

'That is – his plan is wonderful, isn't it? Really – when you think. So we must thank God for that. I really mean it... Even how I'm going to die. Will I suffer? I ask God in prayer now, so that I may stand it: "O God, give me courage, give me strength for that".

'So, what do you *need*? You cannot take anything with you. It is certain that you cannot take anything out of this world. But even when some people reach old age – they are still wanting everything. They *have* – and yet they want more. I can't understand what for! I say, what you have, give away now – while you're still living.

'I ask God to show me what to do with my money. I don't know how long I'll be here. If God hadn't brought me to England, I wouldn't have been able to help my people at a time when they needed it.

'Only my soul will live on. As for the rest – nothing. You go back to dust – you go back to ashes. What's that? No meaning in it. My body is of the earth – earthy. You die – that part of you is finished. Only the soul lives on to meet our Maker. Yet, praise God, we can look forward to having a perfect resurrection body, in Christ, in Heaven (1 Corinthians 15:49).

'After the 1939–45 war, everything was in a mess and we had to clear up.' As she is thinking so much now about the end of the world she says: 'Towards the end of the world – the whole world is in a mess. The young are being taught rebellion (even children are taken on demonstrations etc.). Any young person can search for God and righteousness – it's good if they can get those things *taught* to them and get these truths into their brains.'

* * * * *

Not long ago, Ma Ma Hta wished to give the School for the Deaf in Rangoon a monetary gift. The school has been given into the care of the Anglican Church in Rangoon. She was invited to present it personally. Military officials of the government were invited to receive it. They would then present it to the Anglican Bishop of Rangoon – for the School.

At the ceremony, Ma Ma Hta did not realise until the last minute that it was customary under the current military regime, for anyone who did a good work, such as donating a fair amount of money to a good cause – to be photographed and for an article to be written in the paper, to encourage and reward the donor (so that others may do the same). She was really concerned about this custom when applied to herself. The last thing she wanted was publicity. She prayed: 'O Lord, I don't want to show off. They'll see me in the papers. Please,' she pleaded, 'please do something about it.'

At the ceremony the Bishop stood to the left of her and the two officers in uniform to the right. When she looked at her gift (of money) on the table, she was appalled to see 20,000 *chetts* written boldly on the front of the large box to be handed over! She was mortified – but smiled broadly.

When she looked at an evening newspaper all she could see was a very small article in the right hand bottom corner of the front page. There was no photograph. Apparently, the photographer had arrived late at the newspaper office – so the editor only had space for a few words!

* * * * *

Thinking of a photographer, the author is reminded of the recent marriage of Babs's daughter Kay, Ma Ma Hta's great-niece.

On the wedding day the nave of the church was filled with guests and local friends representing 46 nations. As the bridal procession came down the aisle after the ceremony, *there* was Ma Ma Hta looking strong and well, in beautiful Burmese dress, her hair swept up in a chignon style – looking years younger!

The reception was in a marquee in the grounds of a National Trust stately home near Rowlands Castle. Ma Ma Hta sat surrounded by her closest friends, including two ladies from Burma whom she had known from childhood, one now a widow of a Burmese Ambassador. The lively Royal photographer, also seated, entertained them throughout the meal addressing them as 'Girls'. Even late that evening as Ma Ma Hta walked back through the grounds to the tune of loud calls from peacocks, she was still overflowing with joy.

* * * * *

Ma Ma Hta thinks now that the Lord has put her into the situation where she has everything, and at the same time has nothing.

Compared with the great suffering of the believers written about in the Bible – her small 'suffering' amounts to nothing. 'When you think of *Christ* – our sufferings are *nothing*.' As she leaves the future in God's hands, she quietly looks forward to Christ coming again – to earth.

Appendix

Note A: Rangoon City: 1941

Driving into Rangoon one goes along the Prome Road through rubber plantations, and twelve miles of pleasant, straggling suburbs. Passing Inya Lake – Rangoon's Reservoir – used for boating, swimming and island picnicking.

On, to the American Judson College, and the University, in parkland. (Whilst in Burma, the Japanese would choose the latter to be their Army Headquarters). Beyond it are the homes of the wealthy. Further on – Royal Lake, Botanical Gardens and Zoo.

One passes the railway station, as traffic builds up towards the city centre and flows around the Sule pagoda. In this area is the stone City Hall – also the cinemas. There are many tree-lined roads for hundreds of people walking between shops, offices, houses, the High Court, the Secretariat, schools, the General Hospital and Medical College; also hotels, restaurants, clubs, several sporting facilities; and workers making their way to and from the factories producing ice and soft drinks, shoes, candies and artificial flowers etc.

At the Rangoon riverside there are Customs Houses, Offices and the well-established Grand Hotel (which the Japanese Naval Command made their Headquarters).

Driving eastwards, the waterfront is crowded with boats. Further along are the docks, with ships and craft of numerous shapes and sizes – ancient and modern – packed together alongside the wharves. (By 1941, Burma was the chief rice-exporting country of the world.)

But what about the most famous tourist attraction in the land! Driving back, through the centre of the town, past avenues of flowering trees – past the Governor of Burma's Residency (near which is Ma Ma Hta's workplace) – past the Dufferin Hospital for Women – towards the western suburbs. A mile-long avenue of stately palms and other graceful trees, leads to an incline, approaching the gigantic, gold-encased Shwedagon pagoda. It stands on a fourteenth-century site – upon a low hill (as most pagodas do). At 360 ft this one is said to be the tallest on earth.

Some report that the *Mons* pagoda, built at Pegu, while being repaired after the 1931 earthquake, was made a *fraction* higher – but all agree that the Pegu one is not as magnificent as their *Burman* Shwedagon. Encircling its massive structure are 64 smaller pagodas, in two rows, painted in red lacquer – each one containing a statue of Buddha. This is the main shrine of the Buddhist religion and a place of pilgrimage.

Writers on the Rangoon of that time, vary in their views:

C. Maxwell-Lefroy (*The Land and People of Burma*) writes that Rangoon had 'tall, stately buildings of white stone and red brick', and was 'one of the finest, cleanest cities in the east'.

Another thought that it was the 'least' Burmese town of any. (A great number of Burmese liked the city.)

Leslie Glass (*The Changing of Kings*) describes the town as having 'ugly Victorian buildings' – adding that 'it was not Burma'. He went on to write: 'Only the Shwedagon pagoda which floated over the town gave promise of a more mysterious and beautiful interior' of the land of Burma. Because of the peculiar shape of the structure – from certain angles, and in some lights – the Shwedagon does look as if it is floating above the trees.

Rangoon was a pleasant and some think exciting city in which to live – though, sad to say, not all that *Burmese* in character or atmosphere. In the eyes of visitors, the nationals appeared to be surrounded by foreigners.

In 1939 the population was almost one million. At least half were Indians who had been drawn by prospects of employment as city clerks, servants, coolies, dock-workers and for business reasons. The British, Chinese, Europeans and a few Americans with those of other nations, were there for business, educational, medical, missionary and military reasons, or for civil administration. Others had found it attractive enough to settle there.

In 1851 Burma was ruled by those of the British Raj in Delhi and regarded as a province of India. Rangoon was little more than a village of muddy tracks and teak or bamboo houses along the riverbank. There was little trade up and down this tributary of the Irrawaddy.

In 1854 – after the 2nd Burma War with the British – it grew into the city of 1939. As exports expanded, the harbour was enlarged. Business had been built up by, in particular – English, Scots, Indian and Chinese entrepreneurs. Rangoon had become the centre of commerce and industry for the country.

Note B: The Governor and Political Change: 1941

In Rangoon, there was one particular person who knew the dangers of the current military situation throughout the land: no less a person than the British Governor, Sir

Reginald Dorman-Smith. Prior to the Japanese raid on the
city, he had put into action various contingency preparations towards improving all available defences. (Ma Ma
Hta had seen him and his wife on more than one occasion
– at official functions and annual Festivals, and also at the
School for the Deaf, in which he was genuinely interested.
The school was near Government House; he gave all the
deaf children special leave to play in his beautiful garden,
and invited the Girl Guides to camp in the grounds.)
The Governor exuded warmth. He held a real affection
and sympathy for the *Ludu* (common people), as did his
consort, Lady Dorman-Smith.

   Glass writes of the Governor: 'He had an understand-
ing and friendship with ... (the Burmese), and understand-
ably some feeling of obligation towards the powerful pre-
Japanese Occupation (young) Nationalist Leaders of
Burma, to whom Aung San and his comrades were "the
Boys".'

   Until 1941, most Burmese nationals had been working
with their elected Government, though comparatively
few had chosen to join the Army or the Police Force. In the
1920s, there had been demonstrations in Mandalay; in
1930, a serious rebellion in Lower Burma. In 1936, a University strike disrupted the capital, with further demonstrations. Yet at that time, most people were said to be still
'affectionate towards the British' – so says Glass – 'It
would have been impossible for a handful of Britons to
have governed the millions in India and Burma without
the close co-operation of local nationals in all aspects of
administration and without the broad consent of the
masses.'

   Since 1937, when Burma had been given Home Rule
after the elections, the *same* national political parties had
been in power. These were: The General Council of Buddhist Associations, the Myochit (Nationalist Party) and

the 'Synyetha' (Poor Man's Party) which fought for Burma's independence from the British.

Now, in 1941, the National Leaders, who also had much experience of practical administration, were:

U Chit Hlaing, U Ba, U Pu, Dr Ba Maw, and U Saw.

Glass also noted a significant point, that, 'After 1937, *Burmese* Ministers had ... effectual control over practically all the Internal Affairs of the Country.'

By 1941 the Japanese had reached Siam (Thailand). The situation for Burma was potentially dangerous. The Governor sought to protect the Burmese people. He worked unstintingly to keep before the United Kingdom Government the pressing needs of Burma – making a special effort to bring home to the UK Members of Parliament the urgent military requirements of the British colony.

The Prime Minister, Winston Churchill, however, and the Cabinet (including sympathetic Heathcote-Amory) – *also* faced a prevalent need, in several other countries; and needed to defend Britain herself. The UK Government was trusting in Singapore's military strength and preparedness for the defence of British interests in the *Far East*.

At this particular period of World War 2 – the following facts would not have been of any comfort to the Burmese, if they had known them:

1939–40 (1) The battle of Britain was on. Germany had bombed major industrial cities in the UK including London, for 73 nights.
         (2) The Battle of the Atlantic was on, with great loss of shipping, food supplies, armaments and war-planes
         (3) Britain, with reinforcements from Commonwealth countries, had single or joint military commitments in 13 countries, plus

some of the southern European states, and
was sending military supplies to the USSR.

In 1941   UK Income Tax was 50%.
                 War Expenditure – £11,000,000 per day.
                 (In 1997 this would be approximately
                 £30,730,150 per day.)

The Governor of Burma knew that several extensive areas
of the country were going to have to be very poorly
defended – unless something was done at once. Other
political leaders at this time considered that the Japanese
would attack *India* by sea, but the Governor believed that
they would probably make for Burma first.

Note C: The Invasion

Shortly before realising that the Japanese were ready to
invade Burma – to attack India – Winston Churchill
arranged reinforcements for Burma through the Com-
mander-in-Chief in India, General A.Wavell – who dis-
patched troops and armaments to Burma and sent his own
Chief of Staff, Lt General T.J. Hutton to take Command of
Defence, Rangoon. Churchill promised men and supplies
after the North African Campaign had been won against
the Germans.

The Japanese were on the eastern border of Burma.
There were only two British Burma Army Divisions in the
country – 17th Indian along the 400-mile frontier with
Siam and 1st Burma in the Rangoon district.

The Governor, upon military advice, made a speech on
BBC Radio, Rangoon to the people of the city to strengthen
them and prevent their morale from being destroyed after
the city's second bombing. His listeners were supportive.
It is reported that many citizens behaved magnificently.

Glass writes that among these was a 'gallant Burmese lady: who had personally set up a Depot for the Issue of Free Rations' for any left destitute in the remaining population, after the raids and the outgoing of the refugees. 'Her name was Daw Mya Sein.'

The main spearhead of the Japanese forces began the invasion in the south, crossing the border at Victoria Point. In Tenasserim State, internal communications were poor. They devised a method of warning of the Enemy's movements. Enthusiastic local people, in the tallest trees, day and night, had given signals the moment they spied Nippon aircraft or soldiers. These signals were taken up and passed on at record speed. Due credit was given to them for a job well done. Nevertheless, the Japanese were able to march in, without opposition, in that region.

The biggest surprise – to the Burmese citizens – was to see the recently-formed *Burma Independent Army*, of about one thousand men, heading the columns of the Japanese Imperial Army. It was led by thirty young nationalists, including Aung San and Bo Ne Win (Bo means General, or Military Leader.)

(The above Army was not the *Burma Army*, formed years before by the British who enrolled Britons, Karens, Kachins, comparatively few Burmans and Chins, and Gurkhas. Included with the Burma Army's administration, were national women of the Women's Auxiliary Service, Burma, later to work as cypher staff at Army HQ at Shwebo.)

After the southern invasion, the Japanese crossed the eastern border, swarming over the hills like single-minded ants. They cut off 17th Division, inflicting heavy losses. Gen. Hutton sent help. American General Joe W. Stilwell, commanding Generalissimo Chiang Kai-Shek's 5th and 6th *Chinese* Armies, advanced south-eastwards, fighting well, but in the end, collapsing. The remainder joined the Burma Army on the Irrawaddy.

The Governor was making a tour of Burma, by car, to keep the Burmese people calm.

The Japanese spearhead took Moulmein but was delayed at the demolished bridge on the Sittang River.

March 5th 1942 – Singapore fell to the enemy. There were many reasons, but one is not usually mentioned. It has been said that Singapore Island's water had been cut off: it used to be piped from the mainland of Malaya.

Burma's main body of defending soldiers – Burcorps (Burma Corps) – commanded by Lt Gen. 'Bill' Slim, battled desperately for four months in the hottest weather, in the plains of Central Burma. They suffered many privations – including sickness and starvation and a small minority of Burmese deserters. They were unable to do more than put up a rearguard action – to protect the thousands of civilian refugees on their escape routes to India, and to prevent the Japanese from getting through to the Indian border before the expected heavy Monsoon rains began. Many gave their lives. Lt Gen. Slim led his troops from Prome, north of Rangoon, to Mandalay, fighting all the way.

April 1942 – The Japanese broke through on the Irrawaddy where the British were defending oilfields at Yenanyaung. The enemy had air supremacy and was bombing all the main towns. The retreating British blew up the oilfields.

Already, there were reports of Japanese bestial treatment of their prisoners of war. (Lt Gen. Sir W. Slim wrote, in *Defeat unto Victory* – that amongst the British, Indians and Gurkhas, there were 'rare cases where prisoners were not seriously mistreated'.)

During this crisis period, most senior Burmese civilian officers stuck to their posts and were loyal to the British. Someone has written that the best civilian Intelligence Officers were the up-country members of the business firms who had close knowledge of Burma and its people.

Ma Ma Hta and the teachers and pupils from the School for the Deaf were up north in Mohnyin, during this time.

Note D: Burma – Education in General

During the period when the British ruled Burma – up to 1948 – in the mainstream schools, primary and secondary education was in English. Ma Ma Hta's father taught in English. This applied in the British and American-run schools. A few Burmese schools of this type had come into being, where the teaching was in the pupils' national language. By the 1920s, '.... the Burmese themselves built up 23 national schools with grant systems', writes Norma Bixley (USA). University, College and Technical College education was in English. There were only two universities in Burma – both in Rangoon: first The Judson Christian (American) College, followed by the establishment of the British Government University.

Children of pre-school age could attend the small, local, private schools to speak in Burmese, or town schools that taught in English.

Schools known as the *hpongyi-chaungs* (monks' schools – for boys) had existed throughout Burma through the centuries. By 1930, mostly because of the consistent teaching done by the monks, at least one-fifth of the population could read and write in Burmese up to second standard. This was a high proportion when compared with other eastern nations of that period.

The British, with the eventual co-operation of the monks, introduced a small number of additional subjects, besides the Buddhist-based ones studied in the *hpongyi-chaungs*.

The British made a law forbidding Christian over-proselytisation in the English-speaking schools. They considered that it might give the Burmese parents the idea that the Government was interfering with Buddhist religion.

According to Norma Bixley (1988 book – *Burma*): 'The Burmese people had ... a general respect for learning.'

Before the British came, Burmese women held a particular position in society: they had no formal schooling. A few of the rich or educated could give their daughters tuition.

'Their womanhood and its position in Buddhism kept them out of the circle of the monasteries and therefore of the *chaungs*.' Boys in the *chaungs* were regarded as novice monks: they alone could enter the monastic order.

'Only the monks themselves normally became Scholars (scholarly), with certain outstanding exceptions ... i.e. gifted men at the Court' (of the Burmese Kings).

This was all before the monarchy came to an end in Burma, in 1886, when the last Burman King, influenced by his own Queen Mother, ordered the drowning (traditionally by tying in a weighted sack and dropping into the river) and demise of a great number of his relatives – in fact, every possible Pretender to the throne. The British banished him and his Queen to southern India. The other tragic thing about all this was that the last monarch of Burma had not appeared to learn anything from the fine example of his illustrious father, who had been the pious and highly educated King Mindon.

Bixley also informs us that when the Japanese were to occupy the country, general education virtually ceased (but some of the rural areas were completely bereft of a teaching monk, because monks had evacuated).

In 1942 the British staff in schools, colleges and the university had been ordered by the Governor to evacuate – as were teachers of other nationalities such as Americans. A few chose to remain. During the war, any educators, of any nationality including Burmese, who were still in situ had to rally round to do what they could to continue the education of small groups of children, privately.

Before the war, during British rule, the English-speaking schools were in towns. It was not easy for a Burmese-speaking village child to pass from a pre-school local education into a town English-speaking Middle School. The village parents had to make sure that their children were educated in English at an early age, and attended a good Primary School first. Once having grasped the English language, these pupils benefited, especially higher up the scale, by being able to cope with any available University literature worldwide.

Note E: The Trek

Capt Hla Thin left Ma Ma Hta in Sagaing. He travelled to Shwebo, Gen. Alexander's HQ, where British troops were gathering to march over the Burma border into India.

The Captain saw hundreds of military wives and children being taken in vehicles to be replaced by boats, and more vehicles, to carry them to the foothills, which they would climb. He marched out of Shwebo with the last contingent of soldiers – 110 miles through the malarial jungle of the Kabaw valley, under sporadic bombing and strafing by the enemy.

Crossing the Chindwin river in small craft, as the main body of the army had sunk larger vessels (550 sunk there, and near Mandalay some to be refloated when the British returned during the Second Burma Campaign), these last of the soldiers then marched across a dry plain until they toiled up the bordering hills, some rising to 5–6000 ft.

Collis writes of an incident that happened at the very beginning of the British Army's evacuation: Signals'

wireless operators were 'generally in communication with
the east bank of the Irrawaddy forces ... (but) an atmo-
spheric freak gave them London instead ... They heard the
Archbishop of Canterbury praying for them ... that the army
would come safely out of Burma! ... Throughout the long
march, they experienced nothing but kindness in the
Burmese villages except in one held by rebels.'

The governments of both India and Burma had
dropped supply dumps of groundsheets, blankets, tents,
waterproof sheeting, medical supplies, water and food
along the Tamu escape route (and other routes further
south). Elephants were used for carrying children and the
weak, and for bearing supplies backwards along the track
to the places where they were needed. The Monsoon had
broken, making tracks slippery. People who were soaked
could become ill; mites and mosquitoes brought diseases.
The soldiers, who had been fighting non-stop for months,
were malnourished, many had fever and were wet
through, day and night, with torrential rain.

Captain Thin was comparatively strong physically, as
he was not long out from India. But he was unwell and frequently hungry and thirsty, though he caught a little
water in his hat or drank from uncontaminated mountain
streams. Some died by the wayside, but not as many as on
the Tamu route. Vultures were vigilant.

Ma Ma Hta told me of one particular experience of Hla
Thin, while on trek:

'One sunny break-in-the-clouds, Hla, who was desperately
thirsty, was trekking alone when he came abreast of a British
couple who had lived for many years in Burma. They spoke
to him, so he thought he would stay with them for a while.
They talked of many interesting things and it was obvious
that they loved his homeland. They had been pleasant to this
national but when the lady stopped for a little refreshment

and he sat down a stone's throw away from them, he sensed a change in their attitude. What had made the difference? After some time, the husband lit a fire with wet sticks, and they made a small pot of tea (which Hla didn't realise would be their last). Then he heard the man whisper, "Let's give him some," but that was met with the words, "Why give it to him!" – in a disparaging voice – "Anyway, we've only got enough for ourselves. We have to survive!"

Capt Thin was touched to think that the man who was in such a dire extremity had thought of him, and he wanted to show his gratitude. The only thing he had was a small printed Union Jack flag. He went over and offered it to the lady as a gift. She was delighted and asked if he would like a cup of tea. The Captain graciously accepted. He did not say that the flag was his Army Intelligence Corps (SOE) identity tag!'

The refugees nearing India were met by teams of medical and administrative staff with food and water. Once in Manipur State, they were given transport. Hla Thin was in a very poor condition physically: he also suffered from the effects of malaria. Sent from Imphal to a Calcutta Hospital for a check-up, it was months before he was able to return to the SOE work.

The bulk of the army took three weeks to trek in: 200,000 soldiers and civilians poured over the border into British India, arriving by May 20th 1942. India did its best to accommodate and cater for them all.

Note F: Burmese Attitudes

By 10th May 1942, the Japanese held most of Burma.

The country was in a chaotic, anarchic state, so it was decided by the Japanese that the people should be ordered to go back to their own villages, towns and cities. The orders, couched in friendly terms, told the populace that no one need be afraid: the Japanese Imperial Army was there to save them from the colonialists. They gave the impression of being conciliatory, suggesting Burma would soon be independent.

Obviously, the people could not be expected to suddenly take to the Japanese – even though they were Eastern rather than Western. The writer, Maurice Collis, who saw things more from the governmental point of view, maintains that the Burmese: 'knew that the Japanese were committing suicide because of America's strength'.

'They expected the British to return ... Even the hill tribes knew that the Japanese would have to be beaten in the end.'

'Many liked the British – but (some thought) it was and should be "Goodbye".'

'Asia rejected the Japanese ... expected their defeat.'

Collis explains that after the defeat and exodus of the British, the Chin Hill beyond Kaleymo and the Kachin Hill tracts to the north still belonged to the British.

Later, it was found that many Chins and Kachins were staunchly pro-British and subsequently supported them until their re-entry into Burma.

Glass appears to see the attitude of the Burmese from a slightly different perspective. He regards their attitude to the Japanese invasion as one of being still 'friendly and courteous' to the British. 'There was no nationalist uprising behind British lines ... no anti-British manifestations anywhere in the countryside ...' 'The ordinary up-country peasant saw with bewilderment and apprehension, the collapse of the *Asoya* (government – in this case British) ... felt no particular sympathy for the Japanese invaders.'

Ma Ma Hta comments: 'Most of the Burmese were still loyal to the British.'

Note G: Burma's Wartime Provisional Government

By the end of 1942 the Japanese were telling the Burmese that their future was with victorious Japan. They announced that Burma was now an 'Independent State', but the people knew that it was the Japanese who ran the country, although the government had all the appearance of a dictatorship. During the Occupation, there would be no legislature and no democracy. Any action taken without warrant could be immediately rescinded – for 'Military Expediency'. The Japanese Army ruled.

The Japanese leaders went on to instigate the idea of 'The South-east Asia Prosperity Sphere' and they urged the people of Burma to think of themselves as part of the whole of SE Asia, who would work together with other countries for the good of all. They wanted them to look less to the Western sphere.

At the same time, they expected the Burmese to feed the vast numbers of Japanese soldiers, who had entered their abundantly fruitful land. The people had to provide the army with rice, fish, meat, fruit, milk, poultry, eggs, sugar, and oil for cooking – on demand. This eventually meant that every national was at least reduced to half their normal rations: many had to survive on less.

As for the Provisional Government in Rangoon – in August 1942, the Japanese had appointed U Ba Maw to be the Head of the Executive and had given him the title: *Naing-Gan-Daw Adipati* (the latter means Leader). They seemed to think that he was loyal to Japan – but he knew that two members of his government were going to India to obtain aid for a Burmese Resistance Movement.

Maurice Collis gives us an idea of the kind of Head of State this Premier would turn out to be, during the rest of the war, in Burma:

'Ba Maw did not crawl to the Japanese. He was not a mere yes-man ... he stood up to them ... took risks to tell them unpalatable truths ... turned a blind eye to what the *Thakins* (Burmese government Independence leaders) were doing'. He himself was not a Thakin, but acted as their ally. It was two of these Thakins who were to walk over the border into India to seek military aid in their fight for Independence (against the Japanese). The head of the 'British-born' embryonic Burmese Resistance Movement was soon to be Than Tun and his second in command, U Mya. They were to receive an official Indian Government promise of small arms, explosives for sabotage and money etc. The potential Resistance work was kept secret from the Burmese population. Meanwhile, U Ba Maw was beginning to play his role admirably, maintaining an atmosphere of comradeship while amongst the Japanese and deliberately giving the impression that he was co-operating with them!

According to Collis, Premier U Ba Maw, also kept up a certain amount of pressure on the Japanese Wartime Commanders and their Government in Japan. He later went with a group, which included Aung San, to Tokyo – to discuss 'true Independence'. The Japanese promised it but, upon their return to Rangoon, the Burmese were only advised that there was to be a new Constitution.

By February 1943 – HM Government (UK) offered the Burmese provisional government a draft Plan: there would be a period of direct rule by Britain after the war – possibly for five to seven years – during which the war damage done to Burma would be restored. Following that there would be *Independence* – Burma being given Dominion Status within the Commonwealth – and free elections to a Parliament. The Burmese provisional government stipulated that the direct-rule period should be one year. The UK Government did not fix dates. Britain increased its efforts to regain Burma. (Some remote hilly regions of the country were *still* under British control.)

Note H: Allied Military Efforts: 1943

During 1943 – while these things were taking place in the Bassein area – in India, military preparations were going ahead for the Second Burma Campaign, to retake Burma:

1. Eastern India – build-up of armaments, men, women (mainly Medical Corps), along 700–mile Burma frontier. Airstrips, roads, constructed by tea plantation workers and others.
2. Gen. Joe Stilwell's vision – the Ledo Road – was being gouged out of borderland hills and eventuallly extending through northern Burma – to join the old Burma Road (to China), with American machinery and Indian and Chinese workmen. An oil pipeline fixed to run from Calcutta into Burma. Troops training in Jungle Warfare.
3. Army, air and naval Services stretched to the limit. Shortage of men, transport and food. (Europe was the war priority.)
4. Arakan (SW Burma) invaded, abortively. Japanese reinforcement 54th Div. plus part of 55th under Lt Gen. Kanabe ceased hostilities when the Monsoons started.
5. Col Orde Wingate and *Chindits* – first incursion into Burma. Flew in by glider, behind Japanese lines – for sabotage work. 10,000 did not return. (SOE working in Burma too.) Low troop morale – but world's press blazoned *Chindits'* exploits, and brought hope.
6. Delhi Conference – British, Americans, Indians, Chinese, Dutch Military Leaders – under Admiral Lord

Louis Mountbatten (Supreme Commander South East Asia Command).

Combined Operations to oust Japanese from six Far Eastern countries (including Burma).

General Sir W. Slim wrote later: 'No one could fail to like the Supreme Commander.' He was Head of thirty Military Departments, each headed by a General. Before vital decisions – agreement necessary with Roosevelt, Churchill, Chiang Kia-Shek (China), and General Wavell, Viceroy of India. Had to know world strategy and world politics at the time. (Headache – enough supplies.)

7.	In India	Army: XIVth Army established (Lt Gen. Slim).
		Navy: Combined Operations. To help with landings and supplies. Many vessels sent to Europe.
		Air Force: American/British Combined Ops were to be a unique factor in the Burma Conflict – by air supply galore.
	In Burma	Radio propaganda aimed at the Japanese was being heard, from Delhi. (Prepared by the British.)
		Burmese-style Newspaper and Leaflets – dropped. Truthful news – good and bad. In one, showing Gen Maha (Buddhist hero) in traditional armour standing up to the Japanese. (Stirred Burmese national spirit.)
		Resistance Movement: receiving help from India.
		The Japanese were getting ready to invade India, feigning an attack from the Tamu Pass area (but planning a main one further north).

Note I: British versus Japanese: 1943

One of Winston Churchill's tasks was to 'defeat Japan on the mainland of Asia'. To that end SEAC was formed – August 1943. (South East Asia Command – comprised Burma, Ceylon, Siam, Malaya, Sumatra, Fr. Indo-China: HQ Delhi, India). Churchill chose Admiral Lord Louis Mountbatten to be the Supreme Commander (Air, Sea, Land).

Feb 1943 — The British began harassing the Japanese in Burma:

(a) SOE — Special Operations Executive, Force 136 Calcutta: gathered intelligence, dropped behind Japanese lines, organised Burmese guerilla bands, provided aid to the Burma Resistance Movement.

(b) Arakan attack, S W Burma – aborted.

(c) By Apr 1943 — W Burma, Chin tribal irregulars harassed the Japanese. Trained by British, they 'were better armed and led ... were doing well' (Maurice Collis). 'Further north ... Kachins were also fighting for us.' Karens joined the saboteurs.

(d) Feb-Mar 1st incursion of Brig. Orde Wingate's forays behind Japanese lines with his *Chindits*.

June 2nd incursion, supporting General J. Stilwell (USA) in his conquest of extreme northern Burma to reopen land communications with China, with the object of B-49 bombing of Japan from there. (Governor Dorman-Smith in UK, acquainting British government and public by films of Burma's plight.)

(e) Aug 1943   – SEAC formed. Lord Mountbatten's
                priority – retake Burma.
(f) 2nd Arakan attack in preparation
                (successful in Feb.1944). British had no
                idea that the Japanese were planning
                cleverly for a major offensive into India
                (Mar 1944).

Japanese versus British 1943

(a)   Japanese main tactics aimed at taking India.
            Concerned they should be unhindered by the
            Burmese population. Suspected existence of a
            small Resistance Movement; sought to gain
            the trust of all Burmese.
(b)   Arakan Monsoons fiasco. Japanese told
            Burmese their future was with 'Victorious
            Japan'.
(c)   To keep Burmese happy:
    (i)   Japanese announced Burma 'Independent';
    (ii)   Supported Burma National Army (outwardly);
    (iii)   Allowed entirely Burmese (provisional,
            puppet) Government.
            (Japanese military rule at all levels.) The
            Burma Government: Head of the Executive
            Ba Maw.
(d)   Japanese duped by Ba Maw; led to believe that
            government and people were behind them.
            He risked keeping Thakin Resistance Move-
            ment a secret. He appointed four Thakins to
            government (Resistance leaders).
(e) 1943   Japanese sent massive reinforcements
            from Pacific islands' losses.

Note J: January – September 1944

During the events in chapters 7 and 8, the following was taking place: the British and their Allies (in India) were short of military supplies. Attacking the Japanese in S. Burma by sea was impossible. Naval and amphibious landing craft were removed from the Indian Ocean to the south of England for the 'D Day' landings in France.

June – *Gen Joe Stilwell*(USA), leading the Chinese, advanced southwards in Burma – to take the northern town of Myitkyina (main Communications Centre) and also the airfield. Slow advance, stiff opposition. The General said, re conditions: 'Rain, rain, rain; mud, mud, mud, typhus, malaria, dysentry, rotting feet, exhaustion' (Gen. Slim's book *Defeat unto Victory*). Gen. Stilwell took Myitkyina.

1. British Army – to weaken Japanese Defences in Burma 1944:
  (a) SOE, Calcutta – Intelligence, behind Japanese lines; aid to guerillas.
  (b) Delhi Radio – breaking down morale, e.g. news of Japanese losses in the Pacific.
  (c) Psychological warfare:
      Burmese-looking leaflets dropped by air encouraged nationalist feelings. Truthful news of war gains and losses given. Burmese trusted them. Also leaflets in Japanese, revealing inside knowledge of specific faults, in named Japanese Army sergeants etc. undermining trust in their leaders.
  (d) April – 2nd second incursion of *Chindits*.
      Long-range air penetration behind Japanese Lines. Americans dropped supplies. – Railway lines cut; airstrips and strongholds made. Many *Chindits* killed. Maj. Gen. Wingate killed, aircrash (March).

Mar–July – Japanese huge Reinforcements.
2.(a) March 15th Japanese Invasion of India. Infiltrated through north-western hill tracts. Attacked *Kohima* (Assam): 13-day siege. British Indian Army, including Burmese officers, prevented gain of link road.

(b) – Imphal: 64-day siege. On the Imphal Plain – huge army stores, ammunition dumps ready for Burma campaign. Also airstrips. (Capt Hla Thin was there for a time.)

Japanese short of military and medical supplies and pack animals. Rains began. Starving, sick and exhausted troops fled to Burma leaving a few of XXXth Division to fight to the death. One British Officer, Maj John Raynar, who survived Imphal siege said, 'It was touch and go. The Japanese almost took Imphal.'

One figure for Japanese dead is 53,000. Their General committed suicide.

Note K: April – December 1944: The Japanese

April – Burmese short of food and commodities: multitudes of Japanese fed off the land of Burma. There were no properly functioning hospitals and no medicines, bar Burmese herbals. Little rice cultivation. No cotton goods for clothing. Burmese still arrested, tortured, shamed by Japanese face-slapping etc.

May – Japanese unaware: Governor Dorman-Smith in UK making suggested post-war plans for Restoration of Burma and 'to put forward the miseries of the Burmese to the UK Government' (Collis writes).

June – Aug – When the British XIVth Army re-entered

Burma the UK Government gave Dorman-Smith more detailed plans for compensating Burma.

Lungling Battle: Japanese lost large portion North Burma to American, Chinese and British forces. (Gen. Joe Stilwell's Chinese troops were helped by the British, who had re-entered Burma and recrossed the Chindwin river.)

Northern Burma – the vitally important *Ledo Road* was being strengthened (supply route from China to Burma). American Brig.Gen. Pickard was in command of the loyal Indians, Kachins and Naga peoples in the north-western hills. Without the knowledge of the Japanese rulers of Burma, these men were equipped and ready for guerilla-like action.

Sept – The British had supremacy on the ground and in the air – but the Japanese fought in such a way that the Allies had to kill every single Japanese defender before they could advance even one mile! The British had a good foothold in different parts of Burma – but they had no idea what difficulties lay ahead: of the severe privations, fiery conflicts, and intransigence of every single Japanese soldier.

Gen. Sir William Slim, Commander of the XIVth Army, said:

'They had a fanatical will to resist'. Small groups of Japanese literally dug themselves into the hills and it took a long time and a lot of ammunition to deal with each group, with many Allied casualties. Gen. Slim also wrote that they 'had a capacity for suffering'. In one place, after the pounding of Japanese positions – he and his men witnessed the last few survivors emerging from their dug-outs and to the amazement of the Britishers, they got themselves into order – to march down to the river to drown themselves (rather than suffer the untold indignity of being a Prisoner of War).

Quotations from *Defeat unto Victory*.

Sept – U Ba Maw went to Tokyo a second time – just before the full-scale Second Burma Campaign – to earnestly request the Japanese to withdraw their forces from Burma. He wanted to spare Burma another invasion. The Japanese refused to do so.

It was at this time that Aung San sided positively with the British. The Japanese Commanders in Burma were soon to have the *Burmese* people behind the now well-established guerilla movement.

The Japanese had much to contend with:

1. Northern Burma –
    Chinese Divisions under Gen. Stilwell and three Chinese Generals. (Later advancing down the eastern side.)
    The northern hill people.
    The American Air Force was in action in the north.
    The XIVth Army entered Burma over the north-western border, covered by the American Air Force.
2. Central Burma –
    The Royal Air Force was responsible for the covering fire for the British XIVth Army, which was advancing eastwards, and towards the south and Rangoon.
3. Southern Burma (Arakan) –
    The RAF was also covering ground troops there, as they sought to advance over the jungly Arakan Yoma Hills, to get to the Irrawaddy. (Arakan was taken on August 3rd.)
4. Disaffection –
    The Burmese Provisional Government Underground movement was working in co-operation with the British. The general population that realised the situation, had a attitude of passive resistance; they were united against the Japanese – damaging roads, doing

sabotage work, and even killing individual Japanese when an opportunity presented itself. U Nu persuaded the Head of the Kempetai (Secret Police) to take on three Burmese men, loyal to Burma! They tried to confuse the Kempetai, causing them to believe that there was hardly any disaffection in the country.

Nov – Japanese air attacks were so fierce and almost constant, that the British had to move by night.

Dec – The Americans had to withdraw all their air support, because the planes were urgently required by Chiang Kai-Shek, in China. In Burma, the XIVth Army fought continuously for 10 months – in 1944.

Note L: Second Burma Campaign and Victory: 1944–45

By Aug 1944

(1) General Burmese population passively resistant to the Japanese.

(2) One National Resistance Party in government; political parties had amalgamated – in resistance to the Japanese: *Fabia Mahabama* – the Great Burma Party.

Mid-Dec 1944

Chinese Armies captured N E border town – Bharno.

Late Dec 1944

British had direct and supportive contact with Burmese Resistance Movement (British Intelligence SOE, India).

The Japanese only had three armies left plus reserves.

Jan 1945

British XIVth and Allied American/Chinese Army reached Shwebo. (Capt Thin left it in 1942.)

Mar 1945 – Mandalay re-taken.

Meiktila and several other key HQ towns with ammunition dumps etc. captured.

Mar 1945

(1) Bogyoke Aung San plus Burma National Army leave Rangoon for the 'Battlefront', marching to the jungle where Aung San announced *'We are at War!'* (*with the Japanese!*)

(2) Recognised officially as an Ally, by the British.

Apr 1945

British XIVth Army 'Race' for Rangoon:

(1) No boats, airstrips, railway rolling stock – at first.

(2) Army vehicles were driven along the railway tracks towards Rangoon.

The Burmese made great efforts to thwart Japanese advance.

Committed acts of sabotage; gave misleading information etc.

Chins and Karens especially, did many heroic deeds.

Apr 24th 1945

Japanese Supreme Commander ordered his forces to hold Rangoon.

May lst 1945

An RAF reconnaisance pilot saw words on roof of POW jail: *JAPS GONE. EXDIGITATE* (RAF slang – hurry up). He landed and visited prisoners!

May 3rd 1945

The British entered Rangoon.

General Sir William Slim wrote that the Burmese gave the XIVth Army 'a grand welcome'.

Bassein – the last town in Burma to be reclaimed.

May 7th 1945

General Surrender (Europe).

May 17th 1945

UK Government sent White Paper on Burma:

Admiral Lord Louis Mountbatten met Burma provisional Government and Civil Affairs officers to explain the Policy: Three years British Direct Rule (Military Rule; then handover to a freely elected all-Burmese Government); Burmese Council to be restored; Burmese Legislature also; General Restoration and re-building in Burma (at the UK's expense).

June 15th 1945

Victory Parade, Rangoon.

June 20th 1945

Governor Dorman-Smith's speech to Burmese leaders abroad HMS *Cumberland*, explaining the White Paper in more detail.

July–Aug 1945

Burma General Election

Aug 6th 1945

First Atomic bomb – Hiroshima

Aug 9th 1945

Second A-Bomb – Nagasaki, Japan

Aug 12th 1945

Japanese Surrender

END OF WORLD WAR 2

Note M: Adoniram Judson, 1788–1850: American Missionary

(Notes compiled from Sharon James' book on Mrs Ann Judson)

Father – Congregational Minister. Adoniram a brilliant young man, became an atheist; converted to Christ 1808. There were no Missions other than to the American Indians. Judson and three friends were given the vision for the world. Consequently they were sent to the East by the

newly appointed American Board of Commissioners for
Foreign Mission. Mr Judson arrived in India – became
convinced about Baptism – and he and his wife thought
they should offer their services to the American Baptists
(Mission) 1812. The Judsons arrived Burma 1813.
Proselytisation forbidden. The few British Baptists, who
had begun the Burmese language work, soon retired,
prematurely; Adoniram was able to use their initial notes.
He translated the Bible (helped by Burmese people) into
Burmese, by 1834; also producing a Grammar book and a
Dictionary 1849. Imprisoned during the Burma-British
War. (Ann had died 1826.)

The work of reaping a spiritual harvest (18 Burmese
by 1822) continued at great cost to Adoniram himself –
including the death of his second wife and several of his
children. He became terminally ill.

Sharon James quoted Wayland's words: 'The impor-
tance of his work to millions of immortal souls was ever
present to his view... the revelation of the most High ... and
a heavy weight would have rested on his soul if a single
idea in the Scriptures had been rendered obscurely'
because of 'haste, impatience, negligence or ... ignorance
on the part of the translator.' Judson read much Burmese
literature to help him to understand the Burmese mind.

A distinguished linguist in India, thought that Judson's
translation of the Bible was 'perfect as a literary work'.

One Hall of Rangoon University bears Adoniram
Judson's name. He is still remembered with respect by
both the Burmese and Burmese Christians.

ERRATA:
Sir San C. Po (DR.) was Burmese.
Stanstead House, Near
Rowland's Castle
Town, is privately owned.

Bibliography

The Bible: references (Revised Version)

Borderlines: Nicholl, C.: Secker & Warburg

Burma: Bixley, N.: Praegar, N.Y., 1988

Burma, Myanmar: Klein, W.: Edit. J.G. Anderson: Insight Guides: APA Pubs.,1988.

Burma: Hoskin, J., Text: L.I. Tettoni, Photos: Times Travel Library

The Changing of Kings: Memories of Burma 1934–1949: Glass, L.: Pub. P. Owen

Defeat unto Victory: Slim, W.J., Gen. Sir: 2nd ed.: Cassell, 1956

Elephant Bill: Williams, J.H.: Doubleday, Gdn.City, N.Y., 1950

History of Burma: Harvey, G.E.: 2nd ed.: Bombay, Longmans, Green & Co., 1947

History of the Second World War: Vols 1–6 (Official Records): Edit. in Chief, Capt Sir Basil Liddell Hart: Edit. Barry Pitt: Purnell & Sons, London, 1966

A History of South East Asia: Hall, D.G.E.: St Martins Press, N.Y., 1968

The Land and People of Burma: Maxwell-Lefroy, C.: A. and C. Black, 1963

Last and First in Burma 1941–48: Collis, M.: Faber & Faber, 1956

Myanmar (Burma): Wheeler, T.: Travel Survival Kit: 4th ed.: Lonely Planet Pubs., Oct 1998

My Heart in His Hands: Ann Judson of Burma: James, Sharon: Evang. Press, 1998

Tour & Explore Guides: Waitt, P.: E. Asia Handbk, Moorland Pub. Co., 1988

36, Canterbury Court,
Station Road,
DORKING RH4 1HH

OUT OF THE COMFORT ZONE

George Verwer

ISBN 1–85078–353–5

Reading this book could seriously change your attitude! George Verwer has managed to write a book that is humble and hard-hitting at the same time. He doesn't pull any punches in his heart's cry for a 'grace-awakened' approach to mission, and wants to cut through superficial 'spirituality' that may be lurking inside you. George Verwer is known throughout the world as a motivator and mobiliser. *Out of the Comfort Zone* should only be read by those who are willing to accept God's grace, catch His vision and respond with action in the world of mission.

OM
publishing

OPERATION WORLD

PRAY FOR THE WORLD

Patrick Johnstone

ISBN 1-85078-120-6

The definitive guide to praying effectively and specifically for every country of the world, formatted for daily use, or to dip into when praying for missionaries or around current events. Using this book is an excellent way to involve yourself in global mission.

STOP, CHECK, GO

Ditch Townsend

ISBN 1-85078-364-0

Anyone planning on going overseas on a short-term missions trip should soak up the contents of this invaluable book. Helping them to prepare practically, personally and spiritually, this superb book will ensure that the benefits of the experience are greatly increased to all concerned.

OM
publishing